EMPLOYERS VERSUS EMPLOYEES

Vladimir John

MERIGLOBE ADVISORY HOUSE

2018

Publisher © 2018
MERIGLOBE ADVISORY HOUSE Ltd.

ISBN 978-1-911511-52-6

Vladimir John

EMPLOYERS VERSUS EMPLOYEES

52 STORIES
ABOUT HOW
EMPLOYEES
TYPICALLY
TRICK
THEIR
EMPLOYERS

CONTENTS

THE MOUSE PROBLEM

I decided to start this book in a relatively unusual way: with a story about something that happened to me and that, however amusing or banal it may seem, actually says a lot about the different approaches of employers and employees.

At the beginning of my entrepreneurial career, some thirty years ago, my parents gave me a house in a small town. It was rather a spacious house, so, being a business rookie, I used the ground floor as my offices. I furnished them and hired new employees.

One autumn day, I came back from an out-of-town appointment and wanted to reply to some client orders. As soon as I arrived, several female employees swooped on me with questioning and scared looks. I thought they were having a serious work problem, but I was relieved to discover that it was just a mouse hiding somewhere under the furniture. However, I didn't yet know how much of a problem it would become.

Logical thinking

Without much excitement, I asked some manly members of staff to catch the mouse or at least chase it away. Having made the request, **I considered the problem solved** and asked my employees to get back to work.

If you happen to have a mouse in your house, what do you do? Quite logically, you catch it – you take care of the problem – and I expected the same from my employees.

Two days later, I asked them about the mouse's fate. But I got no clear answer. They said they hadn't found it, it had probably run away.

Everyone makes their own odour

However, a couple of days later, an unpleasant odour started to waft throughout the ground floor of my houseO. With a great deal of irony, I told my employees that they must have underestimated the success of their mouse hunt and I left for a meeting.

I expected that the smell **would motivate them** to find the rodent in its state of decomposition and throw it away. After all, they spent most of their time in the office, so it was in their own interest to sort out the problem.

To my great surprise, when I returned I could now smell a mix of dead mouse and several perfumes in all the offices on the entire ground floor. Again, the employees said that they had failed to find its remains, so they had tried to improve their work environment by spraying perfumes around every now and then.

What I could smell was awful. I thought again about whether they would solve the problem the same way in their homes, but I concluded that since I was often away on business and they were the ones who had to work in that atmosphere, they should bear the consequences of their actions. I expected that they would eventually come to their senses **and figure it out**.

Avoidance instead of minimal effort

I was wrong – again. My employees started coming up with all kinds of ideas, just to avoid having to be in the office. I've never heard so many inventive excuses!

Fortunately, the smell completely disappeared after several weeks and everything went back to normal – even my employees' work performance.

When I was moving the office to a building in the city centre that I hired some years on, I started clearing the ground floor myself. I was astonished to find a dried-up mouse under the smallest and lightest cabinet that was just next to the entrance door.

What is the lesson to be learnt?

- I didn't get it immediately, but after some time I realized how **symbolic** it was. The little dead mouse at the beginning of my business career was a warning to me of what I could expect from my employees in the future. **My company doesn't belong to them; that is why they behave this way** in almost all cases and situations.

- This scenario actually taught me to be more thorough, not to underestimate supervision and not to be afraid to manage people in a more severe manner. Since then I have always demanded clear results from my employees and I don't settle for "perfume spraying".

INTRODUCTION

Every employer's dream is to have perfect employees. That means hardworking people who are reliable, punctual, loyal, honest and resistant to intrigue, corruption and temptation in any form one can think of. If you have luck and good intuition when picking them and happen to find such human treasures, then you should cherish them and be sure not to take them for granted.

You are more likely to come across employees who are far from perfect. It isn't disastrous to have employees who **don't use their brains when working for you, but whose efforts are in line with their salaries**, as they say. But this book does not deal with such employees. Here the focus is on employees **who need or just want to improve their situation at others' expense: and who do so deliberately**, often with almost incredible sophistication. Sometimes they improve their situation at the expense of their colleagues, but most typically they do it at the expense of their employer, that is you.

Such employees may seem to be decent people, and you would never guess they are capable of anything like that. You wouldn't even imagine that there are so many creative ways such people can achieve their mischievous goals. When you read the stories I've written for you, you'll probably be taken aback by some of them, wondering whether anything like that is actually possible. I'll tell you straight away: yes, it is!

Donald R. Cressey, a US criminologist and sociologist, created the world-famous **Fraud Triangle** (Figure I.1) theory about dishonest employees. According to the theory, there are three conditions that lead to fraudulent behaviour: ***motivation, opportunity*** *and* ***rationale.***

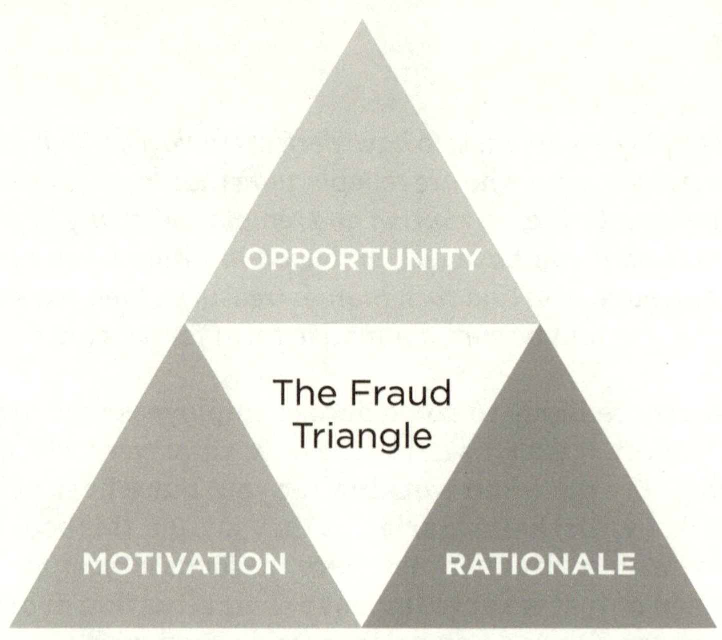

Figure I.1 The Fraud Triangle

It is interesting to look into the figures from the latest research conducted by PricewaterhouseCoopers that surveyed what led employees with no tendency towards fraudulent behaviour to eventually commit fraud. In more than 70 per cent of the cases it was motivation, or pressure if you like, exerted on such people. Opportunity was the decisive factor in only 15 per cent of the cases and the ability to excuse their behaviour (rationale) in 12 per cent of the cases.

David T. Wolf and Dana R. Hermanson later complemented the triangle theory with a new factor: **capability**. That means that employees have to be capable of committing the fraud – with respect to their job position and, for instance, their intelligence or talent for lying. The result of their theory is the **Fraud Diamond**, shown in Figure I.2.

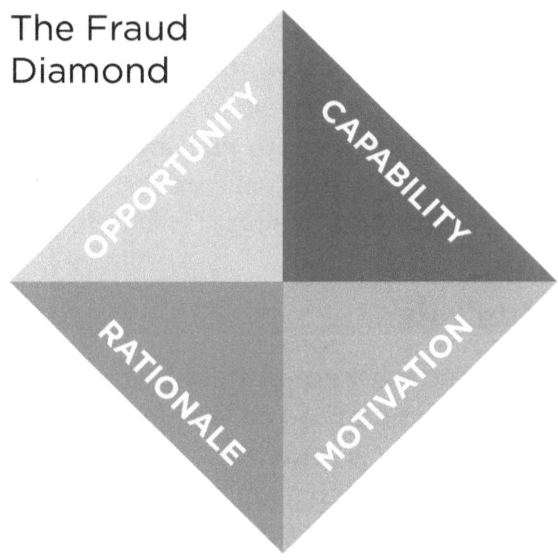

Figure I.2 The Fraud Diamond

At least the part that concerns employees' competences and job-related conditions is fully in the employer's hands. The other factors need to be watched out for by supervising and checking all your employees: in other words, it is about knowing and being ready.

WHY THIS BOOK IS FOR YOU

This book is intended primarily for entrepreneurs and employers. It should warn you of the risks related to dishonest employees, and – more importantly – help you recognise such employees in time. As I have mentioned, the fraudulent palette used by employees is varied almost beyond imagination, but fraud is often linked to typical features: those that can help you identify and reveal such employees.

Most of the risks can be prevented if you take appropriate measures. When you know what to look for and you notice warning signs early enough, your employees will have a hard time carrying out their dishonest intents. So, you should be as cautious as you can. And this book will help you to prepare.

Statistics don't lie

According to generally accepted statistics, **every second employee** is capable of damaging a colleague or the company they work for as long as there is something in it for them. It doesn't matter if the companies such people work for are state-owned or private, the principle of "what is yours is not mine" applies across countries and political regimes.

And there is a great variety of things that can be stolen, from bathroom soap to ideas and company money. Similarly, there are many ways of cheating employers, from the seemingly innocent faking of an illness to forging documents to thoroughly thought out team corruption.

Learn from someone else's experiences

You might think I'm far too harsh when talking about employees, but my conclusions are based on many years of business experience and many stories of things that actually happened. I'm going to tell you more about some of them in this book.

You might shake your head in disbelief when reading them or shrug your shoulders, or you may even find some of them funny. It is very likely they will give you answers to your own business problems. They will bring you closer to being able to recognize a perfect employee, and if you are really lucky, you may find that you already have one or two such employees.

In conclusion, I'm going to sum up the most important ideas that you will encounter in the book and outline some important advice that might come in handy when looking for good employees or tracking down the bad ones. Anyway, I hope that you find between the lines of the following true stories exactly what you need for your business.

Chapter I

Perks of the job – seemingly innocent thefts

As I don't want to scare you away with catastrophic scenarios right from the beginning, I've decided to start on a lighter note with something that some may consider just a minor offence. Well, unless they've happened to experience a similar situation with such "imaginative" employees. In that case, they would call it what it is: theft.

Even very "minor pinching", as is common among employees, may grow from the appropriation of seemingly trivial things such as a pen, a couple of envelopes or several sheets of office paper into vast damage that will significantly affect the employer's economic situation. As everyone knows: the more one has, the more one wants!

Smugglers

Some employees seem to be so modest and inconspicuous that it would never cross your mind to suspect them of doing anything dishonest. The contrary may be the case. As the good old saying goes, sometimes the darkest place is under the candle flame. The following story will take us to Italy, but the truth is that it could have happened anywhere. Small-time thieves like Angela and Roberto, the main characters of the story, are to be found all over the world.

I would like to use this story to demonstrate that people can steal virtually anything, and although such theft may seem a totally negligible trifle at first, it may later result in something much more serious. Small things can add up to something big, if accumulated day in and day out.

When you learn of the life story of the two plunderers, you might feel sorry for them. Well, as long as the things they steal don't belong to you!

Place: **Italy**

Main characters:

Victim no. 1: owner of a dairy **Victim no. 2:** owner of a meat processing plant	**Employee no. 1:** Angela, working at the dispatch department of a dairy **Employee no. 2:** Roberto, working at a meat processing plant

Newlywed troubles

You may find this story amusing or even absurd. One really doesn't often encounter a match as perfect as Angela and Roberto certainly were. Their symbiosis rested mainly on **how they could strategically supply their kitchen through their joint efforts**.

The young couple was at the beginning of their relationship. Neither of them was earning big money and they had been living in a rented flat for just a couple of months while discovering what it took to live on their own and the expenditures of running a household. They often didn't have the money to pay for a proper meal, let alone enough to furnish their new love nest.

As is well known, love can move mountains, so it was out of the question that they would give up on that. Together they looked into ways they could effectively reduce their household expenditure. It didn't take long before they realized they had the solution within arm's reach – literally.

The incessant defiance of discreet Angela

Angela worked in the dispatch department of a dairy. In fact, she spent her working days in a kind of big fridge where she had to wear a lot of clothes so that she didn't bring home a cold along with her wages, let alone some more serious illness.

That's why she, just as most of her colleagues also did, filled a thermos with hot tea every morning and brought it along with her to work, as it kept her warm throughout the day. Everyone found it normal and logical; the security guards knew about it, so it never occurred to them that they should check thermoses.

When leaving through the company gate, Angela had her moment of small daily defiance. She would always **pour milk into the empty thermos** at the end of her shift **and take it home with the satisfaction of a job well done**. Employees were actually allowed to consume as much unpacked food and milk as they liked at work – but they were not allowed to take anything away.

At the beginning, Angela had a simple justification: if she hadn't brought the tea in the morning, she would have drunk the milk that she was entitled to all day. So, it was actually hers; she only drank it at home and shared it with Roberto. Logically, the employer couldn't possibly suffer any actual loss, she thought.

Once she had completely quietened her conscience, she tried to improve her smart plan a little. She realized that when she filled the thermos with cream cheese instead of milk it lasted longer and she and her boyfriend saved more money.

With this ingenious trick, she took home **all the other kinds of dairy products** she had to hand. She could carry them away in her thermos and remain entirely unnoticed. She didn't get caught, not even a single time. The security guards didn't care about the presumably empty thermos in the slightest. After all, every employee had one.

The difference between the amount of goods her employer made and the amount shipped was getting bigger and bigger. During their working hours, employees consumed almost **20 per cent** of their average salary.

As a result, the employer's salary costs grew by 20 per cent and **consumption of dairy products at the workplace eventually had to be banned**. A new employee was hired to check other employees' honesty. It was a very cheap option and, what's more, it increased work efficiency. Employees had to work harder when supervised and couldn't afford to have snack breaks that often.

A small snitch by inventive Roberto

Roberto, who was working for a small privately-owned meat processing plant, wanted to keep up with his partner. With both of them having modest incomes, every little bit helped. Since Angela took care of the dairy products, Roberto's task was obvious – being the man he had to bring home the bacon!

Roberto's primeval hunting instinct was strong. He just had to figure out how he could take meat from the factory without getting noticed. It was easy for Angela with her thermos, while Roberto would look weird with a thermos at work and he couldn't fit a leg of ham in it anyway – maybe a sausage, but that wouldn't be enough for the two of them, and he didn't want to feel outdone in front of his beloved girlfriend.

Roberto was a sly fellow and he found a way. Prehistoric man didn't need any containers either, and the simplest way is usually the most efficient one! So, our hunter decided to **smuggle meat products on his person**. In his mind, he often thanked God that he had got sacked from the bakery. A cool sausage feels much better against bare skin than the hot baguettes he used to carry home before.

In winter, the situation was even more favourable, as he could sneak away much more meat **under his hat**. Roberto was proud that even on days when Angela wrote him quite a long "shopping" list, he didn't let her down and was able to prove his love by always getting her whatever she felt like having.

The young couple economized merrily like this for a long time, **simply because they could**. Because nobody noticed. Once supervision was introduced and a ban on food consumption at the workplace was imposed, Angela considered handing in her notice, but she couldn't find another sector anywhere nearby that would complement Roberto's so well. So, she soon learnt to predict the right moment when the supervisor would pop out or focus on somebody else, and although she didn't bring home as much as before, it was still good enough. And the joy of outsmarting the employer's new system was much greater than before when it was so easy. No one was going to get the better of her!

Previous experience of these modest thieves

If you find this collaboration to be a romantic gesture of cooperative partners who were just fighting for their love, I can tell you that these two people were meant for each other. Each of them did similar things at their previous jobs before they had ever even met.

Angela worked as a stock keeper in a food shop, and she enjoyed a rather varied diet. She never hesitated to eat anything that caught her eye in the store room, and she was masterful when it came to taking small goods out of the shop. The person held responsible for deficits when stocktaking was done was the shop manager who was materially liable – so Angela had nothing to worry about.

Roberto's best memories are of a summer job where he sold fast food on the beach, and he also didn't abstain from eating food on the house. The only thing he regretted was the bitter ending: when the owner found out about it after a month, Roberto was charged for the "lost" food. It was quite a paradoxical situation as Roberto ended up paying more for the food than he had earned. Well, maybe Angela and Roberto were made for each other by a god of food with a great sense of humour.

What is the lesson to be learnt?

The story of Angela and Roberto nicely shows us the basic factors of the Fraud Triangle.

- Without a doubt, both of them had, because of **neglected control mechanisms**, *opportunity*. **The human factor had failed** and the two employees were not supervised. There was no **monitoring** at the two workplaces that would prevent such thefts (although they may seem trivial and harmless until we multiply them by, say, a hundred similarly gifted employees). At the same time, the goods were not protected against theft. So, the opportunity was clearly there.

- Now let's consider the *motivation* for such fraudulent activity. According to the research available, two types of motivation are typical of these kinds of thefts.

1. The first factor is **financial straits** – when employees feel that it is a question of their survival. Employee financial troubles are, according to statistics, at 27 per cent, the most frequent warning sign that you might become the victim of such conduct.

2. The second factor is more prosaic and frequent, **bad relationships between employers and employees** – when employees feel they are undervalued or even being abused. Increased desire for personal profit is directly proportional to how good or bad employees feel at work.

- With Roberto and Angela, it was most probably the first factor, as there are no indications that it would have been the second one. Nevertheless, this feeling that employees may experience goes hand in hand with the last factor – *rationale*. **Rationalising harm** caused to somebody who doesn't value one's work is not that difficult.

Our couple's consciences came to terms with it very easily – they did it for the sake of their love. Moreover, they believed that the employer wouldn't feel such a small loss, whereas it significantly improved their standard of living. And Roberto's opinion on this issue was absolutely clear: could he afford to put his status as a hunter in jeopardy and flop in front of his beloved partner? All men must understand that!

Remember:

- Monitor your employees' movements and activities at the workplace.
- When taking stock of raw materials and finished goods, focus on any inappropriate losses during manufacture, storage and dispatch.
- Observe your employees when they are leaving your premises and perform random checks.

Education, the foundation of life

When someone says "business", most people imagine factories or serious-looking executives in suits. However, business can be done in many various fields; for instance, in education. Now we are going to have a look at a private school where the employees exhibited too much teamwork. The vice of "minor pinching" was very sophisticated there, almost organized.

I am afraid that none of the teachers, who were supposed to be modelling exemplary morals for children and young people to follow, had clean consciences. All of them were doing something illegal, whether it be on a small or large scale. Ironically enough, none of them felt they were guilty of anything. They believed that what they did was absolutely normal and they didn't admit to doing anything wrong. After all, they were doing the same thing as everyone else around them!

Place: **Poland**

Main characters:

Victim:
the founder of the school

×

Employee no. 1:
Henryk, teacher

Employees no. 2+:
most of the teaching staff

A thrifty teacher

Quite naturally, people consider schools to be some kind of holy ground. Teachers are moral beacons, educated people who see their occupation as a mission, and they don't need anything else in their intellectual lives to be happy. Let's meet one of them – Henryk.

Henryk taught Polish at a private lyceum for five years. He was quite a favourite with students, although he was a rather eccentric and distracted fellow. Henryk's friends and colleagues at the school thought that he would remain an old bachelor. Nobody imagined that such a finicky miser with so many bad habits could have a serious relationship. So, when the news that he was going to get married spread throughout the school, it was an absolute sensation.

A nice wedding costs a lot of money

Although Henryk was always thrifty, the sum he had managed to save from his salary wasn't exactly exorbitant. He needed much more to be able to afford a wedding in line with his fiancée's dreams. And he certainly was not going to let his wife-to-be down. The D-day was slowly approaching and the engaged couple were trying to save every single zloty everywhere they could.

We don't know what the future bride did, but let's focus on Henryk, who had a lot of tempting opportunities at school. For instance, his partner told him to take care of the **wedding invitations**. And since she had planned a splendid reception, they needed three hundred of them. Henryk first consulted with a graphic design studio, but when he saw their price calculation, he felt faint. But then he got an idea that saved the day and a lot of money.

He realized they had **a copier at school**. It was situated in an office and teachers were allowed to copy a certain number of documents for students, but that couldn't discourage Henryk from following through with his plan. By printing all three hundred wedding invitations on high-quality paper at school he saved quite a considerable sum from the list of wedding costs. He felt proud of himself. It is all right to do anything in the name of love and, what's more, none of his colleagues could reproach him since all of them used the copy machine for private purposes every now and then, too.

Inventiveness of small-time thieves

As has been mentioned, **he was certainly not the only staff member** who figured out that some money could be saved this way. Henryk was actually inspired by what his colleagues did very soon after he started working for the school and followed in their footsteps. For instance, all of them took home various office supplies; they even took some of the coffee the assistant had supposedly made for visitors. Henryk and his colleagues **didn't consider that theft**. They took everything from "their" school. And who would miss such a small amount of coffee or a few sheets of paper?

Everyone took advantage of what the school had to offer, although some of them **in an exceptionally creative way**. A great example, in this negative sense, was one of Henryk's colleagues: a similarly thrifty soul who lived near the school and took her whole family to the gym locker rooms to shower and use the school's soap. Being a PE teacher, she was "in her territory". And as a woman with a university degree she could easily calculate that doing the family bathing at school was economical, since the school didn't pay the bills for the water they consumed at home.

Even time can be stolen

The other colleagues harmed the employer as well, without actually meaning to. They stole time. Instead of preparing for their classes when they weren't teaching, they browsed the Internet, played games and talked to their friends on social media. They also did some online shopping and had private conversations on Skype or even using the school's telephone. **There's nothing wrong with doing private stuff during working hours, even at the expense of the school using school property, they thought**.

The truth is **they could feel free to do so**. Nobody ever supervised or checked them, nobody reproached them for doing so and nobody told them not to do it. The employer actually didn't ask them to behave differently. Their work contracts didn't stipulate any rules beyond their teaching duties and nobody ever mentioned any unwritten moral rules. If any one of them had any doubts about the correctness of their conduct, they quickly chased such thoughts away. After all, their colleagues were no better and nobody had ever been punished for anything like that – **so they considered it absolutely fine.**

A small affair with a sponsor

Life at the lyceum went on and all the employees were more or less satisfied. Whenever any of them felt they needed an extra bonus, they didn't wait to get it officially. Well, taking into consideration their salaries, nobody could blame them, could they?

Everything was going just fine until one fateful day when one of the sponsors boasted on local radio that he regularly gave this school all kinds of gifts and benefits intended for the students. It was true, the school really did **receive various**

promotional materials, free tickets to theatre performances, concerts, exhibitions, funfairs, water parks and the like from sponsors. However, these never reached the students, the intended recipients.

A few parents happened to hear the sponsor on the radio and a virtual hell ensued. At first they felt wronged because they thought that the other students were the privileged ones, probably due to favouritism. So, they started asking one another about it, and the answer they got from other parents was always the same: no one had ever received any benefits like that. How could they when **all of the gifts and benefits were always taken by the teaching staff**? What the eyes don't see, the heart doesn't grieve over, as the saying goes.

The students and their parents hadn't had the slightest idea that they had been missing out on something for many years. And, of course, the sponsors didn't know that their good intentions meant for students never got any further than the staffroom.

There is an old saying that goes: "There's no escaping fate." The free passes to the swimming pool and sauna mentioned on the radio started an avalanche of parent interest and questions that actually resulted in unexpected hard times for the teachers.

As soon as it came out who had actually enjoyed the donations, it also caught the attention of the local press. The school came under such scrutiny that its teachers didn't dare to even borrow a pencil from then on. Fortunately for Henryk, that happened after his wedding and, with respect to his mean nature, he wasn't planning on any other financially demanding operations, which his wife figured out shortly after the wedding. We can only imagine how the showering PE teacher coped with the change.

What is the lesson to be learnt?

Schools should define clear rules for more than just students.

- **Define** what you consider **unacceptable**, even if it is a trifle such as "free coffee". The best thing you can do is to specify such conditions **in the work contract**, or **in a special agreement** with each employee. The least you should do is define the disciplinary and moral code of your company and display it in a visible place and/or post it on the Intranet.

- Another option is to incorporate the rules into **an employee handbook** that each employee will sign after reading. The rules should be linked to clear **punishments/sanctions** so that your employees know what risk they're running if they breach them. I strongly recommend you hold regular trainings on this topic – for example, every other year – so that all of your employees are demonstrably aware of the rules.

- **Don't underestimate record keeping** and invest in **software with surveillance programmes**. Surveillance software will keep an eye out for all activities that aren't work related on all your devices – and can even prevent them.

This advice doesn't only concern schools. **Procrastination** is actually a phenomenon of the times we're living in and we encounter it on daily basis in every form it may take. I'm going to discuss this topic in more detail in Chapter 13 entitled **Avoiding work like the plague or A championship in procrastination.** You can find more details about procrastination in Appendix III: **Procrastination and precrastination**.

Remember:

- Clearly define which employee activities are unacceptable.
- Outline sanctions for breaching written and acknowledged rules.
- Buy software that will monitor employee activities that aren't work related.

A pressured waitress

The story from the Polish lyceum shows how the total amount of harm caused to an employer grows if more employees are involved and they cover for each other. We can also demonstrate this with the following two examples where a similar collective cohesion turned into outrageous audacity and the provision of "unofficial fringe benefits", even to those outside the given company.

The first story takes place in a typical Slovak pub. There are thousands of them in Slovakia, and there is nothing special about them. The pub is a place where locals meet in an almost home-like atmosphere; where nobody cares if you wear overalls or a suit; where you can have your favourite beer and a nice meal from the daily menu.

At the same time, it is a perfect environment for employees to pull the wool over gullible employers' eyes.

Place: **Slovakia**

Main characters:

Victim: Pavol, restaurant owner	**Employee no. 1:** Valéria, waitress **Employee no. 2:** Milan, cook

Hardworking and irreplaceable

Valéria had been working as a waitress for several years. She was certainly no novice in the restaurant business, and Pavol's pub was the third one she had worked in. She knew the ropes well, so she soon found her feet. The pub's guests were happy with her and she got on well with the owner, whose profit was just about average.

It was only natural that Pavol was satisfied with her work: when he turned up at work, Valéria was very nice and helpful to the guests and her boss, and she rarely took a break. Sometimes she uttered with a sigh that she was rushed all the time, but she **refused Pavol's offers to get her a helping hand**. She said she could certainly handle everything by herself! Why should Pavol pay another employee? She joked with Pavol that he would be lost without her.

Pavol had **complete confidence** in his self-sacrificing employee. He even sometimes asked himself what he would do without Valéria and thought that he could never find another soul as good as her, who would work at full stretch and handle everything by herself without requesting a colleague to alternate shifts with. If only turnover were higher! Valéria obviously had no time to turn around, the place was almost always full and still the pub didn't earn Pavol as much as he imagined it would.

Awakening of a gullible boss

But doubts kept nagging at Pavol. Hence, one day he confided in a good friend who was familiar with the business having previously also run a restaurant. He was much more suspicious than Pavol and offered to help him by doing some mystery shopping. He knew very well what to watch for and how to ask the right questions. None of the staff knew him, so he could go to the pub when the boss was not there. He went there not only for lunch, but for information.

What he found was a textbook example of the saying "When the cat's away the mice will play". At the table where the local patrons normally sat **were six friends of Valéria** who had come to have lunch. They all enjoyed some cabbage soup and *halushky* while drinking beer and lemonade (both of Valéria's children were also there), and then **they left without bothering to pay**.

Valéria's entrepreneurial spirit was obvious at another table where there were two drinkers who apparently were not going to leave any time soon. They seemed to be part of the furniture with a consistently low percentage of blood in the alcohol running through their veins. They had shots, one after another. During the time Pavol's friend was there, they drank their way through half a bottle that, oddly, Valéria kept in the fridge, despite having a cool box full of drinks behind her at the bar. As her boss later found out (surprised by the information from his friend), **she usually sold alcohol from bottles that she was bringing along** herself and all the considerable profit from those sales went into her pocket. She also profited from situations when people invited her to have a drink. She only poured herself a little and filled her glass with ice, or pretended to be drinking expensive Finnish vodka with the guest when she was only drinking tap water. No wonder she didn't want a new colleague who she would have to share her profits with, or who could even betray her.

Pavol didn't know that she already had a partner in crime. She had a very good pact with Milan, the cook, who adjusted portions so that Valéria's family and her friend could have lunch every day for free. Besides that, Milan used to his advantage the fact that his boss wasn't familiar with what supplies were needed for the kitchen. Pavol didn't check the shopping and left everything up to Milan. A large amount of **the food bought with company money for the kitchen ended up somewhere totally different**, not in the bellies of paying customers.

It certainly would have been no comfort to Pavol if he had known how much Milan's relatives enjoyed the stolen food and that it had become a hit at many parties. In addition to cooked food, Milan also sneaked away from the restaurant raw meat, frozen vegetables, smoked meat, cheese, oil and even spices – simply, the things that he needed at the moment or thought he would need soon.

One thief covering for another

Milan knew about Valéria's tricks in the restaurant, and she was aware of his deceit in the kitchen. They had **a quiet unwritten confidentiality agreement**. They sometimes even shared the money they had "earned" and, as they were well acquainted with each other's friends and family, who frequently stopped by to have free food, they often held parties together.

It was a metaphorical stab in Pavol's back. He learnt that both of his employees were cheaters, and he was consequently left without any staff overnight. Not only did it harm him in terms of business, but also personally, as a human being. His confidence in people, after the lesson that Valéria and Milan taught him, was very weakened. He decided not to leave anything to chance the next time and supervised his new employees much more closely.

Another lesson

Sadly, Pavol wasn't lucky with the next cook either. He seemed to be a professional; he had a very good CV and was very skilful in the kitchen. Pavol had also learnt from his restaurateur friend how to check the amounts of food that were bought and prepared so that there was no room for monkey business.

However, he soon discovered that he had hired a drug addict, who **stole the equivalent of his weekly income the first chance he got**. Even before he managed to illicitly get the code to the safe, he had been stealing the empty beer barrels and selling them back to the suppliers. As one could expect, he spent the money on his "hobby".

This experience eventually opened Pavol's eyes fully, and he began to approach his business with less naivety and greater professionalism. He spent much more time in his pub in order to keep a sharp eye on his employees.

What is the lesson to be learnt?

Using this typical, yet quite banal, example I mean to warn you of the truth – that has been confirmed by many real-life stories – behind the saying that **opportunity makes the thief**.

So, whatever field of business you are in, you need everything to run smoothly. If you want your company to flourish, **you shouldn't underestimate control mechanisms**. No matter how much you like your "waitress Valéria", she is still your employee and her interests may differ from yours, quite radically.

Remember:

- Keep in mind that opportunity makes the thief.
- Stick to the motto: "Trust but check". Especially when your employees are in contact with cash, materials, food or anything else they could steal or exchange for lower quality (taking better items home and replacing them with cheaper ones), and so on.
- Don't underestimate the value of constant surveillance and monitoring of the workplace. If you have a larger company, it is a good idea to introduce a "suggestion box" through which any employee can anonymously notify you of questionable practices in your company.

Free relaxation

I promised to give you one more example of how it ends when colleagues pull together too much. We will stay in the same field; we're just going to move on to a higher level of fraud, and the total amount of the damage incurred will also be higher.

In this story, we are, together with the main characters, going to a reputable hotel with four stars. Its owners had great plans and they really tried hard to make it the best it could be. They left almost nothing to chance, but still their business almost ended in tragedy. Why? As the saying goes: look for the people behind everything.

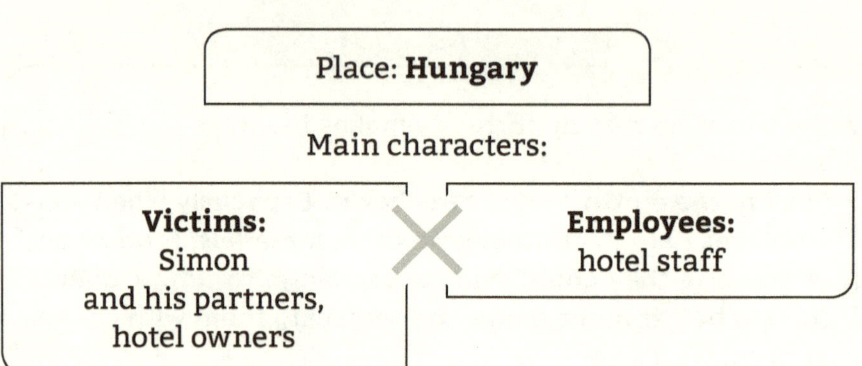

Perfect starting position

When Simon and his business partners invested a considerable sum of money in buying a luxury hotel, they rightfully expected that this transaction would bring them business success. The hotel was situated in a perfect place, far away from the city bustle, and yet guests didn't feel isolated there. The hotel restaurant was well established, the cook was reputable and guests were accustomed to going there.

The new owners thought that the spacious congressional hall would also bring them a lot of money, as it was suitable for holding various events. The indoor swimming pool and sauna were the icing on the cake. Everything was set to be just perfect.

Success did not come

In essence, the hotel was prospering under the new management in a way. It was far from being empty and people were still interested in its services. Clients liked the hotel and the food. They were happy to return, and if they didn't get the chance to come back personally, they passed on their recommendation to others.

The staff were still decent and accommodating, the rooms were clean and cosy, the surroundings were inviting for relaxing walks. There was one event after another in the congressional hall, the swimming pool was always in use, the sauna was heating like crazy. To put it simply, it was a nice and popular place for guests seeking relaxation. The capacity was often insufficient, and they even had to turn people away!

Yet, Simon and his associates came to realise, after several months, that **their profits were far from stunning, considering how busy the hotel was**. There was clearly something wrong. And they decided to get to the root of the problem as soon as they could.

The solution was undercover investigators

The owners realized that the best way to find out what was going on was to be a fly on the wall – to have the chance to watch daily operations unnoticed. And since the staff always behaved perfectly when they were present and they were no novices in the world of business, they knew they had to choose an indirect route.

So, they used the most suitable tool for such cases, mystery shopping, but on a much larger scale than Pavol in the previous story. They asked several of their friends to stay at the hotel individually for a couple of days. While using all the hotel services, they were required to watch what the staff were doing and how they were behaving and then give them a rating from the perspective of a guest. Their impressions were then shared with the owners.

The undercover guests kept their eyes open and even chatted with other guests, most often at the bar where tongues were loose after a couple of drinks. **Thanks to their friends-turned-investigators**, Simon and his associates soon had the opportunity to marvel at a sense of teamwork among their staff that they had never dreamt possible. However, what they learnt didn't make them happy in the slightest.

Perfect collaboration beneath the surface

Not only did their employees take for granted that they could use all the delights and services the hotel had to offer, but they even **invited family and friends** without batting an eyelid. They all enjoyed staying at the four-star hotel or at the very least having a swim in the pool or relaxing in the sauna for free.

That was why, as Simon found out, **the hotel seemed to be full at first sight**. Thanks to the "generosity" of the staff, paying customers often didn't even have the chance to book accommodation. The rooms that were supposed to be available were already taken at a much lower price by a relative or friend, or anyone else who was able to offer the staff something interesting in exchange. The hotel staff cashed in on these people and split the earnings among themselves. Of course, the hotel owners didn't see a single forint of this profit.

They could have been alerted by the fact that **their employees often "sacrificed themselves" and worked overtime**, as could be seen from duly kept records of their working hours.

But as the private investigation showed, **they spent most of the time taking advantage of the wellness facilities**. So, this overtime wasn't beneficial to the owners either.

When patience runs out

Simon and his associates' patience finally ran out on New Year's Eve. The fact that the New Year's Eve party for at least 170 guests, produced a revenue of less than 100,000 forints – around 300 euros – was something they couldn't take lightly or overlook. **They estimated that the loss incurred on that single night exceeded two million forints**, while they were supposed to pay employee salaries that exceeded twice the reported turnover.

As a result, they dismissed most of the troublemakers. However, the after effects of their self-governance were felt even several months later. The owners found out, for instance, that their **enterprising employees had even rented the congressional hall, pool and sauna independently and that the money received went directly into their pockets**. The owners' disillusionment was immense.

You can imagine that they chose their future employees with the utmost care and were determined not to leave anything concerning their business to chance ever again.

What is the lesson to be learnt?

- When **more "enterprising" employees** gang up and cover one another, problems will soon follow. Such problems are hard to discover and they may cause extensive damage. Having **a friendly atmosphere** at work is fine, but **don't assume that it is always a plus**.

- Don't rely on your employees' loyalty. Take the necessary measures to ensure that you have full control over your property.

- Keep perfect **records** of every single bottle in the restaurant and every last hour when your swimming pool is in use, and make use of **technology**: it can keep an eye on many things for you.

Remember:

- ▶ Don't be afraid to use a mystery shopper or a newly hired employee who can help you uncover how the system works from the inside.
- ▶ A friendly atmosphere in the workplace isn't always beneficial to the company.
- ▶ Don't rely unreservedly on employee loyalty.
- ▶ Use advanced IT tools: for cash registers, booking systems, electronic records of your assets and even for opening doors. However, supervision over such systems should be completely separated from the staff, by which I mean you should entrust an outside company to do it for you. Such a company will submit monthly reports highlighting any discrepancies or suspicious activity.

IN CONCLUSION

It should be noted that the employees mentioned in the stories in this chapter certainly aren't the only ones to have ever helped themselves at the expense of their employers.

It has become a sad reality for entrepreneurs that **similar "minor pinching" occurs all the time throughout various fields of business, and it often goes unnoticed**. Sometimes it even happens with the unspoken consent of the employers, as they kind of naturally expect that their employees will find a way to create their own benefits.

But as I said at the beginning of this chapter, and as you have seen in previous stories, the more one has, the more one wants and opportunities make thieves. The end result in most cases is that even **seemingly mere trifles lead to losses in the millions**.

Chapter II:

All that glitters is not gold – the inability to read people

Employees are humans, not machines. You might wonder why I'm writing something that everybody already knows. I'm writing it here deliberately, because I want to emphasize that every person is unique. You need to approach and assess everyone individually. No two people will ever behave identically.

That's why you need to be on guard all the time because you never know what surprise your employees may have waiting for you. So, you should be careful when choosing employees and deciding how much you're going to trust them. The biggest cheaters often excel at feinting. If an applicant seems to be absolutely perfect or even better than you expected, you should be doubly careful to check whether they can really deliver what they promise.

In the following stories, we are going to see how employers who trust their employees too much get tricked, and how it ends when employers don't realize in time that they have a high-quality employee working for them.

A stolen idea

Most of the stories in this book are about employees who are not worth employing. But I'm going to start this chapter with a case of the opposite. As I have suggested, there is a sort of employee that you should recognize in a timely manner and do everything you can to keep them: one who is hardworking, loyal and means well for the company and the employer. However, should they remain unnoticed when there is a more ambitious colleague around, it may easily happen that they eventually get steamrolled.

The sad thing is that you, the employer, may never know that you have lost a super employee, or you may realize it only after it is too late, once such an employee is already with a competitor and you're left with regrets.

Place: **United Kingdom**

Main characters:

Victims no. 1+: owners of a manufacturing company **Victim no. 2:** Peter, a loyal employee	×	**Employee:** Barney, Peter's cunning colleague

No good deed goes unpunished

Peter, a thirty-five-year-old manager worked for a fairly big company on the outskirts of London, was quiet and unassertive, but hardworking and fair to his subordinates. When the company started having financial problems, it quickly became a public secret among the employees. Most of them spent the majority of their working hours discussing the new state of affairs.

Peter was no exception, as the situation looked really serious and he felt responsible for the future of the people working in his department. Unlike his colleagues, who only complained or were afraid of losing their jobs, he wondered what he could do to improve the situation. He thought about all the internal **logistics** until he came up with an idea as to **how they could be rearranged to considerably reduce internal costs and get the cash flow back into the black**.

Peter had a heart of gold. He tried to come up with a solution and he didn't think for a moment about profiting from it personally. He is a typical example of a loyal employee and the right man for the job. Unfortunately, being an introvert who was afraid to talk in public, he wasn't certain whether he could push his idea for a company overhaul forward and defend it in front of management.

So, led by good faith and not expecting anything bad, **he discussed his idea with his colleague Barney from another department**. He wanted to hear what others thought of his idea and listen to their questions and counterarguments so that he could prepare before presenting it to his bosses.

It didn't cross his mind that Barney was not as good a colleague as he took him for – a person who doesn't have treacherous thoughts typically expects the same from others. Barney listened carefully to Peter's suggestions for changing the company logistics, and he shook his head the entire time as Peter spoke. Then he raised his objections, which **threw Peter off balance so much** that he went home convinced he had to rethink, recalculate and rework everything before he dared to present it to anyone. He thanked Barney for being so frank with him and not letting him act rashly.

Victory of an idea thief

Peter was shocked when the following day his colleagues told him that Barney had just been hugely successful in presenting the management with a great idea as to how company health could be improved by adjusting logistics. All the big bosses praised him to the skies because his brilliant plan could be applied immediately and promised a quick reversal of the recent negative developments.

Barney was the kind of person who **didn't want to miss out on an opportunity**. He didn't care about Peter's potential or what he may think about it at all. After all, it wasn't the first time he had done something like this. He had started pretending that other people's ideas were his own when he was at college. His friends supposed he was trustworthy and openly shared their ideas with him, and Barney also won the trust of those to whom he presented the ideas as his own.

True, he eventually lost almost all of his friends, but it brought him success and recognition at work. He climbed the career ladder and earned more and more money. And that's what matters most, he comforted himself. It also worked this time. The management was excited by "his" idea, and the idea thief received – in addition to company-wide acclaim – a fat **extra bonus**.

Peter ended up getting nothing. Being the author of the proposal that eventually led the company out of crisis, he was taken aback. Barney laughed him out of court claiming that Peter's ideas were unusable, while his idea encompassed completely different processes. But Peter could clearly see that Barney's version didn't differ from his in anything substantial.

He fought back his own feebleness and timidity, and the strong feeling of injustice and wrongdoing eventually made him act. He decided he had to **put the record straight and he claimed to be the author of the idea**.

Disappointment, disillusionment and despair

If you thought the story would have a happy ending and that the evil would be punished, you're terribly wrong – provided you wished the happy ending for Peter. **Nobody in the company believed** that such a quiet and shy man could have devised anything so tremendous that it would put the entire company back on its feet. How could he? What was worse, after he revealed the truth, he looked like an unscrupulous person who wanted to take credit for somebody else's idea!

The company management didn't see any reason to question the fact that Barney had come up with the idea and even other colleagues were on his side. It boosted Barney's position, while Peter was left demotivated and disgusted by the tense atmosphere at work where **relationships plummeted**.

Unclear definition of a loss

So how did it end? The idea thief was never found guilty, but he also never came up with another worthy idea. After enduring a couple of days of fuss and doubtful looks all around, Peter decided to hand in his notice. In his next job he proved to be very useful.

Sadly, he was the only one who learnt a lesson from this case and gained something positive out of it. He became more vigilant when it came to trusting others and sharing his thoughts with them. He realized that he had to speak up and stand up for himself when it mattered.

Peter's new employer appreciated his good qualities as well as his approach to the company. If the previous employer had realized the truth, he would have never let him go. But instead they were left with only Barney, the idea thief who enjoyed his fifteen minutes of fame and then became lost in the crowd again.

It's not always easy to decipher the good employees from the bad ones. But if you are lucky enough to have some good employees in your team, you should do your best to avoid losing them.

What is the lesson to be learnt?

You might think that this story doesn't exactly fit in this book. The employer wasn't harmed and, what's more, the company's difficult situation was sorted out thanks to the idea.

That conclusion would be wrong! The employer appreciated the wrong person. The idea thief is not going to think twice the next time he is confronted with an opportunity to trip somebody, for instance his boss.

Another rule for coping with employee risk is:

- If cheaters feel that the **advantages they may gain** exceed the inconveniences caused by possible revelation,

- and if they know that their swindle will be accepted or even rewarded,

they have no reason to refrain from seeking or taking advantage of **another opportunity**. It doesn't matter what their motivation is – whether it is a desire for financial reward, career advancement or social recognition. As has been mentioned several times, the more one has, the more one wants.

At the same time, the company created the **potential for a high-risk employee** – Peter. His future steps and decisions will always be influenced by that unpleasant experience. The primary source of trouble is not always the employee it seems to be.

Remember:

- ▶ When hiring new employees, check their references carefully. Don't hesitate to call previous employers to ask about them. Don't trust the information presented by the applicants!

- ▶ Regularly assess employee work performance.

- Introduce a system for employees to submit innovative ideas electronically or in writing, assess the ideas on a regular basis and reward the submitters.
- Every employee must earn their keep.

A bureaucratic fairy tale

We're going to stick with high-quality employees for some time. We'll just look at them from a different perspective; to be precise, at the relevant risks. You may think this is illogical nonsense – what risks could there possibly be with high-quality employees?

Getting such employees, keeping them and motivating them are what I consider to be some of the most important activities an employer can engage in. I hope that you are able to recognize them so that you know who is worth keeping around and you don't let them go! That is actually the biggest risk – that you won't recognize them and you'll let them leave to work for someone else, or you may even drive them away, although unintentionally.

This is what this story has in common with the previous one, although the course of events is totally different. But even here, the employer didn't know what he had and his inability to read people actually resulted in the loss of a very good employee.

Place: **Czech Republic**

Main characters:

Victim no. 1: Martin, employee **Victim no. 2:** Přemysl, employer	×	**Employees:** Rudolf, HR manager Pavlína, HR assistant Milada, IT manager Jindřich, office manager Veronika, Jindřich's secretary Evžen, auditor

A perfect employee

This story could start out like a fairy tale. Once upon a time, there was a diligent employee named Martin who always arrived at work on time and worked so hard that his boss Přemysl couldn't believe how lucky he was to have him around. Martin was reliable and never complained. He led a small team of people in the manufacturing department, and together they were a well-oiled machine. Martin set an example for his colleagues, there was a friendly atmosphere in the company and everything was working, which is something many employers dream of.

This is where the fairy tale ends, because people often don't value what they have and want more instead. That was probably the reason why Přemysl came to believe that if somebody started supervising **Martin and his team, they could become even more efficient**.

New assets

It wasn't long before Přemysl hired Rudolf as HR manager. His task was, in addition to achieving the highest work efficiency, **to keep track of the attendance of all employees**. Martin was thrown off balance a little to find out that instead of recognition he was given a supervisor, but he carried on with his work and didn't comment on the changes.

While there was nothing Martin could be reproached for, the same couldn't be said about the new HR manager. Shortly after starting work, Rudolf said that there was too much paperwork regarding attendance and asked for an assistant. Therefore, another employee was added to the team: Pavlína.

The company is growing

Přemysl was so enthusiastic about Rudolf and Pavlína's supervision that he wanted **graphs and in-depth analyses of employee productivity**. So, he bought them a computer and printer and hired Milada as head of the IT department.

Although the company had a lot of employees who supervised others and processed statistical data, the manufacturing team was not strengthened by a single person. However, the graphs showed, surprisingly, that the work efficiency wasn't increasing. Quite the contrary!

A direct manager

Instead of doing his job, Martin actually spent a great deal of his time **filling out various questionnaires and forms** that Rudolf, Pavlína and Milada badly needed from him. He was, slowly but surely, losing his zest and fervour. The situation with his colleagues was no better, as they lacked a leader and the entire system that had worked so well for many years had been disrupted. Přemysl's conclusion was that they all needed a direct manager.

The person given that job was Jindřich, who started by nicely furnishing his office, asking for a computer and bringing along a secretary from his previous job. Then he convinced Přemysl that it was necessary to work out a strategic plan for optimizing the production of Martin's department and to survey the work environment.

Inverse proportion

The surveys showed that **the efficiency of Martin's team had dropped, while the department's costs had risen disproportionately**! Přemysl suspected that there was something wrong, which was confirmed when Evžen, a renowned auditor, assessed the situation as dissatisfactory because there were too many employees.

Přemysl thought about it. The only person who had apparently lost motivation and was slowing down the new arrangement by not keeping up was Martin! So, the owner of the company took what he believed to be the most logical managerial decision and dismissed him. Soon afterwards, several other people from his team gave their notice, which was something that Přemysl hadn't expected.

He now faced hard times, with too few experienced workers and a supervisory apparatus that was generating a great part of the costs, but which kept decreasing the efficiency. After some time, Přemysl was surprised to realize that by introducing this bureaucratic philosophy into his company he had primarily harmed himself. But it was too late to get Martin and his hardworking team back. Being a diligent employee, Martin was already faring very well elsewhere, without Přemysl and all that tiresome paperwork.

What is the lesson to be learnt?

- When you are lucky enough to have excellent employees, **don't let them get away**. If their work efficiency drops significantly, you should first try to find out the reason and ask other colleagues what they think the root cause is. This way, you can rectify the situation without losing good employees.

- **It doesn't always pay to be suspicious**. If you give a satisfied and hardworking employee a micromanager looking over their shoulder, they will feel like you mistrust them and doubt the quality their performance, which may **cause their motivation to drop**. Moreover, you risk hiring supervisors who will work towards their own objectives rather than yours.

- **Acknowledge those who do good work**. Create a pleasant work environment for them and let them know you are happy with their performance. Honest employees always respond better to **positive motivation, praise and trust**. Try setting higher targets for them and give them the necessary authority to achieve them within their competences; they might surprise you.

Remember:

▶ Keep in close touch with your extraordinary employees and show them that they matter to you – rewarding them both financially and with praise. As a company owner or manager, introduce an open-door policy: anyone can come to you to share their problems or suggest improvements for daily operations.

- Don't forget about positive motivation. Money is one thing, but don't ignore non-monetary rewards such as praise, employee of the month awards and the like.
- Treat all your employees equally.
- Effectively delegate administrative and bureaucratic work to the employees whose job it is. If you ask a programmer, developer or factory worker to do this type of work, it will always be wrong.

Party animal

Being able to read people means, among other things, that you aren't easily fooled by their acting or charm. Naturally, for some jobs you may need a persuasive, communicative and sociable employee who is able to captivate your customers and win their sympathy, but you should be particularly cautious with such employees so that you don't happen to fall victim to their tricks.

It can easily happen to anyone, and even you may find out that the salary you pay your employees doesn't correspond to the results you get from them. Especially if you give them a job high up the food chain and entrust them with almost unlimited powers while forgetting about control mechanisms, as is the case in the following story.

Place: **USA**

Main characters:

Victim: Tom, owner of a PR agency	**Employee no. 1:** Jack, head of the marketing department
	Employee no. 2: Danielle, Jack's assistant

A charming marketer with clipped wings

Soon after he started working as the head of marketing, Jack felt that he was going to like it at Tom's PR agency. In his previous job, he hadn't had nearly as much freedom. His former employer virtually held him down, as he was a stickler for red tape, adhering to boring rules and requiring decent conduct, who didn't understand that the strongest business relationships are built in a completely different way, not by sitting in a suit and tie in a meeting room.

The boss had swept Jack's best plans off the table calling them wild visions. But is it actually possible to aim low in marketing? After all, that was why Jack had picked this field, because it was particularly about entertainment and the art of manipulating people, which were his natural strengths. And since he felt like he was wasting his talents, he started looking elsewhere.

Tom's PR agency seemed to be tailor-made for him. Tom actually had proved to be the perfect boss for Jack at the interview.

He admitted that he didn't understand marketing, which was why he needed an independent and competent manager with creative ideas. Moreover, after a longer period of stagnation, he was ready to allocate a very significant share of the company's turnover to marketing in order to make it really efficient.

Running riot

Jack was an extrovert and naturally loved social events of any kind. After previously working for a "killjoy", he was ready to enjoy an abundance of such events in his new job. The argument for Tom was clear: **the most important thing for a PR agency is that it has to be seen!**

Jack cast his nets wide and Tom's agency was, thanks to the head of marketing, introduced at every beneficiary soirée and social event that took place within a hundred miles. Invitations started pouring in, since Jack was really something when it came to leaving an impression. He explained to Tom that socializing was the first necessary step to getting important business partners to even bother talking to him.

Reciprocation

Soon it was time for the second necessary step. Jack thought that the agency should hold its own events and invite all potential strategic partners to show them what they could afford! When Tom saw how good his new marketing manager was at organizing parties and how interesting and detailed a programme he could prepare, he curbed his worries and congratulated himself for hiring Jack.

The parties held by their PR agency were always talked about for a long time. There were lots of important guests and winning some of them as regular clients would significantly improve the company's situation. According to Jack, it was just a matter of time, and Tom completely trusted him. He had very little experience with modern marketing, and he was happy he had such a skilful and independent guy at his side.

So, after just a couple of weeks, he entrusted Jack with his full confidence and gave him unlimited authority to use the company's money. Jack was completely free to do as he pleased without having to consult anyone about anything beforehand. He was on cloud nine and confidently assured Tom that he would never regret his decision to let him join their team.

An invisible manager

Jack kept spending a lot of time planning and organizing grandiose events for future clients. He needed to be absolutely undisturbed when preparing them, so he was allowed to work from home. After every party he also needed due rest, which was something that Tom understood and he was always willing to give him paid leave.

As Jack was always one of the last ones to leave the parties, he needed to sleep off his hangover. That implied that he usually switched off his mobile phone for the following day or two so that he could build up energy for another effort in establishing new business relationships.

After several months, Tom realized that he only saw Jack a couple of times a month. Jack didn't even have time when Tom needed to discuss orders that were just about to be placed, or at least that's what Jack said. More and more backlogs piled up; suppliers of refreshments and other party supplies called in more and more, often asking to have their invoices paid – they were still in unopened envelopes on Jack's desk.

Jack didn't hesitate for a second when confronted with this fact: he clearly needed an assistant. And he was definitely going to choose her himself so that the two of them would make a good team. So, Tom soon ended up hiring a beautiful woman named Danielle.

The royal couple

Together they were a really lovely couple. They were the stars of every party, where Jack introduced her to important people in their field of business. Danielle was charming, and they received even more invitations than before. She spent one day a week in the office to answer mail, and she accompanied Jack to various negotiations and events the rest of the week.

The invitations were usually just for two people from the company, so Tom, who had sometimes joined Jack if the parties were held in the vicinity, didn't participate in socializing any longer after the new assistant came.

Sometimes he regretted it – at two such events, thanks to his marketer's contacts, he had managed to negotiate two rather decent orders. These were the first two points scored using this expensive way of establishing business relationships. But Jack explained that it was absolutely inappropriate to work at parties, since there were influential people all around who came to relax. The goal was to leave an impression, not to negotiate a deal. Tom felt almost ashamed of the two "points" behind him, when he heard what a faux pas he had committed and that it had looked almost as if he were begging.

The king is dead, long live the king!

When the accountant told Tom that they had been in the red for the past three months, he felt faint. He was lulled by Jack's promises of mega-orders that were ready to be signed, so he covered the losses from reserves. However, when he asked for an overview of the costs and revenues of the marketing department and he couldn't believe his eyes.

The costs for the royal couple had reached hundreds of thousands of dollars in less than a year, while the value of new orders was a little short of 12,000, won thanks to Tom. Jack actually didn't have time to work; he had to party. He enjoyed a luxurious life and Danielle's company and Tom covered all their expenses.

As it emerged later, some so-called meetings with clients took place exclusively in two luxury hotel resorts and casinos. The receipts for the "business" dinners that indicated the participation of at least five people, according to Jack's claims and the amounts of the bills, were nothing but the expenses of the royal couple who had treated themselves to indulgent delicacies and vintage wines.

For many weeks after Tom parted ways with both of them, he was afraid of every new invoice that arrived. Jack was, thanks to his eloquence, often able to negotiate the postponement of due dates for several months, which meant that the company paid for his bon vivant life long after he was thrown off the throne.

The only positive was that when Tom responded to several invitations to parties made by phone, he managed to arrange some meetings with interesting clients, which was because of his serious approach. During his usual style of business negotiations, wearing a suit and tie and sitting in the company meeting room, he was still shaking his head in disbelief, even while signing agreements. His business partners told him that they had long tried to arrange business matters with Jack, but he had always waved them off to leave it for later, as **it was time to have fun!**

What is the lesson to be learnt?

- There is no place for blind faith in business. Although you cannot understand in detail all aspects of company management, **you should at least have a basic awareness and keep track** of how each employee is working so that you don't let others string you along.

- Especially management positions should be filled **with duly checked employees** with good references and clear motivation. Charm is not the right criterion; on the contrary, you should be extra careful when hiring charming people.

- Don't leave your employees **unsupervised** for long. Even the best ones will eventually slack off if nobody is supervising them. The same applies to management – even managers must produce tangible results.

Remember:

- If you want to manage anyone efficiently, you must know exactly what you require of them. That means you need to clearly define each job and the relevant duties.

- The higher the position your employees hold, the more you should know about what they are doing and motivate them.

- Even if you think you know exactly what's going on, you should still continue with monitoring and regular reporting. They should, for instance, submit weekly reports on their activity, projects, client visits and so on. It is also a good idea to have employees who work out in the field, such as business representatives or employees who take care of key customers, enter standard information and the actual status of agreements into your information system so that you can get in touch with customers quickly if a business rep becomes unavailable (not necessarily because of termination of employment, but, for instance, due to long-term illness). In this case you will know what stage the agreement is at and what has been promised, done or agreed upon.

How not to retire

Do you feel like the inability to read people cannot cause you trouble any more serious than that? Tom lost a lot of money in the previous story, but he entrusted a risky employee with "only" one department. What if there is a day when you tell yourself that you have worked hard enough and that your company is running well and can successfully continue even without you? Do you think it will be easy to find the right replacement who you can trust as much as yourself?

You'll certainly take all the necessary precautions, just as Mark does in the following story, so that you can enjoy the well-deserved rest and reap the harvest of your hard work. You are going to build a team of reliable people and a system that works like clockwork. All you need to do is let go of the steering wheel and hand it over to experienced sea dogs who will navigate your boat through the business waves on a firmly set course straight towards success. What could possibly go wrong?

Place: **Netherlands**

Main characters:

Victim: Mark, owner of a flourishing company, who decided to retire	×	**Employees:** unreliable management

Preparing for retirement

After several decades of very intensively building his company, Mark wanted to finally have a rest. His company was prospering and he wished to retire to a secluded place to enjoy some long-overdue peace and quiet with his family. He was quite right to believe that he deserved it at the age of seventy-five.

He didn't doubt that his company had **such good internal policy and motivational programmes for employees that he had nothing to worry about**. He trusted his employees. He considered them – judging from his long-term experience with them – to be loyal and hardworking.

That's why **he let professional management run his company**. And, under his supervision, they actually ran the company perfectly. All the members of the management team were time-proven employees and the internal bonus programme was a clear guarantee that his successors would take care of his company as if it were their own.

Finally retired

At the beginning, Mark couldn't tear himself away from his company. After so many years of everyday rituals linked with work, it was not easy. He couldn't help it. **He had to show up at his company every now and then**, spend some time in his office that was still there for him, talk to his employees and briefly check up on operations.

Everything seemed to be okay. The world kept spinning. Nothing was going wrong or adrift, even without his intervention. Naturally, he didn't understand every little detail as he had before when he spent ten hours a day in his office. However, he repeatedly made sure that he had chosen the right replacement and that he had nothing to worry about. After a couple of months, he admitted to himself that the company was really in good hands and **he tried to become a full-time pensioner**.

For the first time in the history of his business, he travelled abroad with an empty head and with no worries about what was going to happen. He finally put his company activities aside and did only what he enjoyed.

It was liberating. It was exactly what he had been trying to achieve all his life: to build something great that **he could be proud of and would make him a living** after he retired so that he could catch up on everything he had missed before because of work. His life dream had been accomplished, all he needed to do was to enjoy life!

One in a million disillusionment

As you have probably guessed, there was no rosy future. As soon as Mark succumbed to the illusion of having a well-greased machine that could run on its own, he no longer worried about what was happening in his company, while the carefully-selected, well-trained and experienced **management couldn't care less about his generous efforts to develop a great company** and worked only towards their own ambitions. All of them like birds of feather flocking together.

The managers paid themselves exorbitant bonuses and they hired new employees for the work that needed to be done: the main criteria for new employees were that they were "obedient" and wouldn't have issues with being disloyal to their actual employer. They managed to smartly and inconspicuously get rid of the old and trusted staff whose loyalty towards Mark could have jeopardized them. They contracted new suppliers and sub-suppliers and spoilt the good relationships the company had with long-standing and reliable ones. **After two years, the company had suffered huge losses and its good reputation was becoming a thing of the past.**

Eventually, Mark had to admit that the time to retire hadn't come yet. As soon as he heard the news about his declining company, he immediately ended the longest holiday of his life and **returned to work full of zeal and determination**. It took a lot of effort for **him to get the company back on its feet** and form a new team of people he could trust again. Thanks to them, he could slow down a little later on, but he never completely let go of the reins again. Well, not until he decided to sell the company and enjoy the well-earned money – that he'd had to work for twice – and rest in peace.

What is the lesson to be learnt?

- Even the best **motivational and bonus programmes** cannot **guarantee honest employees**, if they are left entirely to themselves.

- As for **reward programmes**, it has been proved that managers perform better and are more engaged and interested in the future of their company if their **bonus programme is linked to the achievement of long-term objectives**. The European Union has actually endorsed this model as the most effective form of remuneration and motivation for management of banks and other financial institutions. If you are considering a bonus programme for your senior management, you should always **tie it to the economic results of your entire company**, not only to presentations and statistics that can be easily rigged. Assessing performance over a longer term is particularly suitable in situations where clever top management sells, for instance, a subsidiary or other part of company assets, thus improving the resulting balance of the given year and reaching the bonus level necessary, but the following year it is "who cares?"

- Motivational and bonus programmes are good potential tools, but it is still necessary to **continue with control mechanisms** and not to let yourself get disconnected from what is happening in the company. You should keep tabs on the performance and results of **internal as well as external audits** and insist on **adhering to predefined ethical standards** and your company's **anti-corruption policy**. Owners should always keep in touch with key employees, but even ordinary employees should have the chance to talk to you if necessary.

Statistics show that 57 per cent of companies worldwide enforce strict adherence to the anti-corruption policies. For the sake of completeness: the survey involved thirty-six countries from Europe, Africa, India and the Middle East.

Remember:

- The best director of every company is always its owner.
- Don't automatically assume that the directors and senior managers you have hired will be honest and reliable if you don't check up on them regularly.
- The best motivation lies in defining and sticking to long-term goals.
- Use your common sense and don't be fooled by impressive visual presentations and the like. You should always verify data and reports submitted to you by top management. Also communicate with ordinary employees about the situation in your company and ask them what they think about the effectiveness of the internal processes and what they suggest doing differently.

IN CONCLUSION

Being an entrepreneur requires a lot of specific qualities. You need, among other things, to be able to read people. It is difficult to see through your employees, because those who really have something to hide are usually very good at doing so.

Trust but check is a generally valid statement, but when your money and good name is at stake, you are not only entitled to but should feel obliged to be as cautious as you can, and you shouldn't confide excessively in people you don't know very well. If you are not a very good psychologist, you can have your employees take psychological tests – they will reveal any weaknesses and tendencies they may have to try to hide things from you.

Chapter III:

Even paper can lie – applicants under scrutiny

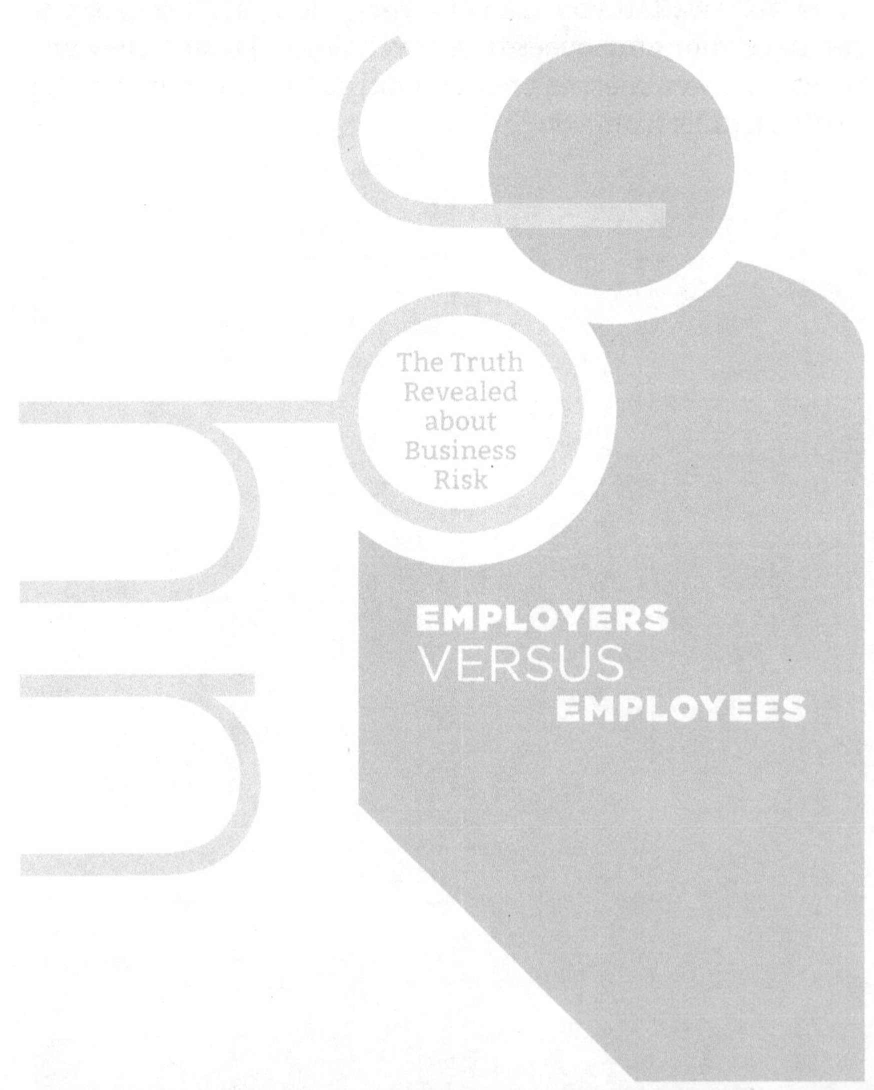

You may be wondering what the title of this chapter is referring to. Usually, we hear that "only what is written remains". Naturally, this is the case with contracts and agreements, but here we're talking about a totally different sphere, and soon you'll realize why I have used this metaphor.

Humans are creatures capable of anything, especially when it comes to earning a living. The audacity of some job applicants is actually unlimited, and it is nothing unusual for ***people to distort or totally fabricate their experience or skills****.*

You should never rely on what you see in an applicant's CV. Statistically, ***every third applicant*** *puts false information in their CV. And 40 per cent of CVs include information that has at least been distorted or embellished.*

Every CV should include references and contact information for previous employers. It is there for you to use and it is not considered shameful or bothersome ***if you ask former employers about an applicant's work history and the reason they left their previous job****. It may warn you in good time.*

Detached branches

It happens quite often. Some people are very good at "selling themselves", and they effortlessly leave a great impression on you. But even if you are totally beguiled by a prospective employee, **it may cost you dearly if you don't bother to check their past**. That is exactly the big mistake the owner of a Danish company made when he hired a nice new employee who seemed to be entirely trustworthy.

The situation was facilitated by the fact that the new employee didn't work **at the company headquarters**, but far from where the owner had his office. The novice got a newly furnished office with all the necessary equipment and free rein so that he could turn all his initial promises into actions.

Working totally unsupervised, the promising employee actually turned out to be a cheater. Or would you call him by another name? You can judge for yourself after you finish reading this story.

Place: **Denmark**

Main characters:

Victims:		**Employee:**
Jarl, co-owner of a company, and his partners	×	Bent, a "dream" business representative

The charm of a new business representative

When a small company decides to expand to other towns or even other regions, it is always a mark of success and shows that the company is faring well. This was also the case of a Danish cheesemaker that was searching for a business representative for their local branch in a remote region who would be in charge of winning new clients and business development.

Jarl, one of the owners, was in charge of selecting the new employee. Out of several applicants he chose forty-year-old Bent. He had excellent references in his CV and interesting past experience. He seemed to be nice and promised very good contacts, many of whom Jarl could imagine having as customers. Since Bent was a natural speaker, he fared very well in the interview. He seemed to be the perfect business representative. The co-owners approved Jarl's choice with pleasure.

A couple of days later, Bent became their employee. He went through some internal training at the headquarters and then moved to where his employer had just opened a new branch. He was supposed to be there on his own for the time being, until the new region started "earning for itself".

As he had to represent his company well, Bent was given a modern office, electronic notebook, telephone, car, company fuel card and a lot of other benefits and tools to help facilitate his start in the terra incognita. As it was obvious that he was **a professional who knew what he was doing**, it wasn't necessary to send anyone along to help him, let alone set up any **supervision or monitoring**.

The owners realized that things were not going to be easy for Bent in that complicated region, and since they didn't want to risk losing such a capable business rep, they gave him a very decent fixed salary for the first six months. They decided that only after this initial period would his salary become performance based.

Waiting for a miracle

Half a year passed and Bent hadn't concluded any deals, but **several new contracts were "just about to be signed", he said**. He described them vividly to Jarl on the phone, and the boss fell for it. Jarl convinced his associates – who were becoming sceptical by that time – that they should subsidize Bent for another three months, as the deals he was about to bring in would make up for it many times over.

After all, the receipts from his branch included high fuel costs and bills for refreshments whose frequency had increased over the past couple of weeks, which corresponded to what Bent had said about finishing his business negotiations.

Patience runs out

But after two more months without closing any deals, Jarl's associates ran out of patience. They were no longer willing to pay for Bent's office, phone bills, business lunches and hundreds of miles driven unless there were clear results. So Jarl decided he would go to the branch in person to check on Bent's performance.

Bent didn't answer the phone for several days. He only excused himself via text messages in which he wrote that he was in the middle of a business negotiation. Later he asked for a couple of days off to recover from a cold.

When Jarl arrived at the branch, unannounced, he was unpleasantly surprised. The receptionist estimated that he had seen Bent there three times at most. So Jarl went to see Bent at home. There he learnt from a chatty neighbour that Bent had left with his family for the mountains in France two weeks ago. She added a few poisonous remarks about how she didn't understand how an unemployed man could kick up his heels so much. She didn't understand how he could afford the opulent dinners and parties that he had been holding at his home for some time.

Unwilling sponsors

But Jarl understood it very well. He called the supposed business partners who all said that they had never heard of Bent or their company. Shocked by how he had been tricked, he called the references from Bent's CV, but they all said they hadn't written anything like that about Bent. They admitted that he had been employed with them, but in most cases they had let him go during the probation period because he had shirked his responsibilities.

As soon as Bent, suntanned and relaxed, returned from the Alps, Jarl challenged him and his worst worries were confirmed. The nice business representative had unscrupulously enjoyed eight months of carefree life, and during all that time he hadn't bothered to do any work at all for his employer. He was like a student trying to enjoy his last holidays to the fullest. The confrontation with Jarl brought a swift end to that.

Jarl and his associates never learnt what reference Bent made up about his employment with them for his CV. But they made sure to check his successor very thoroughly, and the new business representative was under close scrutiny. Their company wasn't going to leave anything to chance and rely on excessive confidence anymore. All the co-owners had quite a decided opinion about such sponsorship.

What is the lesson to be learnt?

- **People can write anything on paper!** The more self-confident a job applicant is, the more cautious you should be so that you don't fall victim to masterful manipulations. The references in the CV are there for you to contact the people who wrote them and check whether the given applicant will actually be the right person for your team. Checking references doesn't mean you mistrust applicants, but rather that you are using healthy judgement and cautiousness that is totally appropriate.

- **Trust but check!** Even if you have employees working far away from your office, there are several control mechanisms you can take advantage of. You need to know that your employees are doing what they are supposed to be doing at the right place and with the right people. That way you can avoid employees like Bent who will otherwise do their business or solve personal matters at your expense and using your assets.

- There's nothing easier than fitting your cars with GPS devices so that you know where they have been used and how many miles they have been driven. Define clearly what purposes the car may be used for, under what circumstances and conditions an employee may use a company payment card, how his or her daily activities will be reported and the like. **Invest in supervisory and information systems!**

By the way, what happens very frequently in business is **fuel leakage**. Oftentimes the fuel doesn't even end up in company cars, but in petrol cans and poured into private vehicles. Another possible scam is **reporting journeys** that were actually never taken, or private travel being reported as business trips. If you own, for instance, twenty passenger cars and all of them are misused in this way, **your losses** may reach, according to the statistics available, up to 10,000 euros per year.

- Another way to prevent the situation described in this story may be to suitably **motivate** employees, making their remunerations depend greatly on performance. **Don't pay for promises, but for actual work.**

Remember:

- Beware that people can write anything on paper, especially on their CVs.
- You need to check employee reports.
- You can use various forms of monitoring.
- Select an experienced colleague to mentor new employees and check their work.

▶ Information systems are there for more than just checking attendance and using basic features. You can also use customer relationship management (CRM) software, which stores information about your customers (including potential customers), the negotiations you have held with them and the agreements you have concluded.

A calculating couple

Another example that should deter you from insufficiently verifying data in applicant CVs is the unfortunate experience of a Polish company owner.

Benedykt was certainly no naive novice. He usually duly checked job applicants' references, and his interviews typically tested the qualities he required from them. Still, even this otherwise circumspect boss underestimated one particular situation, causing big trouble for himself and his company.

Place: **Poland**

Main characters:

Victim:
Benedykt,
company owner

Employee no. 1:
Marián,
business director

Employee no. 2:
Halina,
accountant

An up-and-coming youth pushing his way forward

By the time Marián started working as the new business director, the company had been on the market for three successful years. Its business activities were rather meritorious: it secured cultural and other leisure-time activities for a big Polish city.

Marián soon proved to be a natural authority and to possess great organizational talents. A typical example of the up-and-coming and successful generation of confident managers for whom a career and climbing up the social ladder meant the world.

But he was a thorn in the side of an established accountant, who had been with the company from the very start. She always told Benedykt openly what she thought, but Marián wasn't interested in what she had to say, so after a couple of weeks she decided to retire and leave her job to somebody younger.

Saved time and money

Benedykt wanted to express his gratitude for the accountant's service by complying with her wishes to go immediately without having to work her notice period. So, he rejoiced when Marián recommended a replacement. Marián had worked with Halina at his previous job and sang her praises. He claimed she was a hardworking professional with a great future. And, as if by magic, she was able to start the job straight away.

Benedykt was immensely grateful to his business director. Not having to waste time on the selection process and holding interviews with all the applicants, he could dismiss it from his mind and enable the older lady to retire immediately.

Nobody interviewed Halina before she got the job and the HR manager only checked her CV briefly before filing it. What else should she have done when Halina was hand selected by the business director himself! She must be a very good accountant, there were no doubts about that!

The stamp was still wet

However, nobody, apart from Marián, guessed that Halina had been an **"expert" for just a couple of days** and that the stamp on the certificate confirming she had attended a six-week accounting course hadn't dried yet.

Nobody knew that it was Marián's idea to send Halina on that course so that he could engineer keeping his beloved girlfriend close by, even at work. And he had even enjoyed being rude to an elderly lady in the process.

Working as an independent accountant after just a few weeks of training requires courage and that was certainly something that Halina didn't lack. There would be nothing complicated about it: if an old woman could do it, it would be a piece of cake for her, she thought. Halina thought she would only need to check the accounting folders from the past to know how to go about it. Moreover, her immediate superior was Marián, and she didn't expect the owner to rummage through the accounts.

A masterly plan

Marián and Halina had the time of their lives. They bought each other presents, dined at luxury restaurants and shopped for expensive brand-name clothes. Simply put, they were determined to enjoy it down to the wire. Their salaries, however generous they were, couldn't cover all of that, so they didn't hesitate to take advantage of all the opportunities that their strategic alliance presented.

As the business director, Marián had access to the company's "black budget", which was used to cover expenses that couldn't be considered as direct business costs. It happens sometimes that businesspeople need to invite a client to something that couldn't pass as a tax-deductible expense. Marián used this black budget as a personal "piggy bank", sucking it completely dry.

Later, he started withdrawing money from the company bank account, and he gave Halina the receipts for everything they bought for their own needs: clothes, refreshments, theatre tickets – they always asked for an appropriately phrased invoice and Halina didn't have any problem with adding it to the file with the other bills.

A perfect alliance

Since this method was a little risky, Halina had to become more proactive. The novice accountant unscrupulously dared to issue false invoices and other fictitious receipts from companies and people who only existed in this couple's fantasies.

In a way, it was fascinating what this young woman with no expertise or experience did. Youthful confidence and courage is what she and Marián had in common. Before Benedykt suspected anything, **they had embezzled a total of 100,000 euros**.

When the poor owner found this out, he suffered a heart attack. For an entrepreneur who didn't want to build a company of colossal size, but just wanted to participate in the cultural life of the town where he had lived all his life, it came as a complete shock and was a very bitter pill for him to swallow.

What is the lesson to be learnt?

- This story clearly shows how important it is to **check new employees thoroughly when hiring them**.
- Research has shown that the greatest **risk of losses and fraud**, in terms of financial manoeuvres, is likely to occur if the same person who does the accounting has access to the money. In other words: **the best prevention is to separate the jobs of accountant and "treasurer"**.
- As we have just seen, there can be problems even when the two jobs are done by two different employees who have a close relationship. In order to make sure that this is not the case in your company, **you should perform regular internal audits and emphasize the importance of business ethics in your company**.

Remember:

▶ Watch out for close relationships between employees. Adhere to the four-eyes principle, which means that the factual and financial approvers should never be the same person – these two positions must always be separated. It is of utmost importance that you always sign a material liability agreement with employees who have access to money, company payment cards and the like, and that you set clear rules about how and to what ends they may use cards or money, while requiring that they regularly report all their expenses to you.

▶ Separate couples and family members so that they are not in "superior-inferior" relationships, if possible. If for no other reason than because people who have close relationships give in to each other more than they would to others. And there is, of course, also the risk of them covering up each other's fraud.

- Perform regular internal controls and audits.
- Make sure you have internal regulations in place and check that they are adhered to.
- Even when you are about to hire a new employee who has been recommended to you, require the same documents as when hiring any other employee (CV, references, certificates, etc.). And don't lower your requirements – if a university graduate with certain experience or certification is required for a particular job, expect even recommended candidates to meet the qualifications. Don't fall for their promises that they will prove or complete their education later on.

A robbed diplomat

The following story is more proof that it is risky not to find out more information about a person you're hiring. Sometimes it can **save you a great deal of trouble**, so you shouldn't hesitate to **contact previous employers**. That is why references should be included in every credible CV. The mere fact that the references are missing should be taken as a warning sign and a reason to doubt such applicants.

Especially when you're hiring a new employee for a job in management or a job that requires access to sensitive information, you need to be absolutely positive that such employees are honest and of good character. The higher the position is in your company hierarchy, the more energy you should invest in checking such people's knowledge, capabilities and the credibility of the information they present you with. You could even hire a detective agency that **checks future (as well as current) employees and verifies the information** applicants disclose about themselves.

Egon, the employer in the following story, would have saved much more than the cost of such professional services. He actually thought he was being cautions enough. Sadly, he had no idea that he was facing a very sophisticated and well-prepared crook.

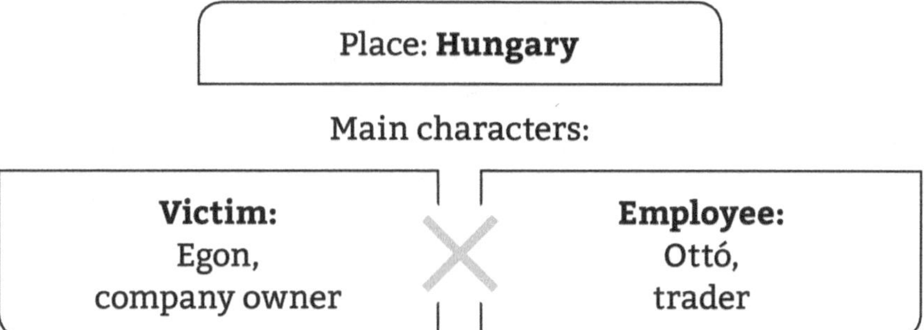

A serious novice

Imagine a nice middle-aged guy who has worked for several years as a diplomat. He looks respectable, is knowledgeable, has connections and good recommendations, speaks several languages, is time flexible and so on. He seems to be **the ideal candidate** in all respects when you're looking for someone to hold negotiations with foreign partners. That was Ottó exactly.

Egon was not new to business and he realized that the vacancy he needed to fill required, among other things, a great deal of responsibility, diplomatic capabilities and credibility, as it would often entail making costly business trips abroad to meet with key clients. Indeed, the success of the company depended on the results of such negotiations. He obviously didn't want to leave anything to chance. Thus, in addition to CVs, he asked all the applicants to submit all their academic certificates, and he **insisted he would check references from their past three jobs**.

Ottó seemed to be a very promising applicant, especially because he spoke fluent Dutch, which was quite rare. Egon's company was trying to establish a promising business partnership in the Netherlands at the time, so overcoming the language barrier would have come in very handy. Ottó was also the right match with respect to his other skills and experience.

He lacked contact information for references in his CV, which Ottó explained by saying that his previous employers were reluctant to disclose their mobile phone numbers and he respected their wishes. However, he said he could make an exception, as Egon and his company had left a very good impression on him. He said he believed that his previous employers wouldn't be upset in that case and he wrote down their phone numbers from his mobile. Egon called all three of them and when they all exalted Ottó to the skies, he didn't hesitate any longer and gave Ottó the job.

Ottó became a promising member of Egon's team, and shortly after his initial training, he went on his first business trip abroad to negotiate with the Dutch customer. As a good level of Dutch language was required to discuss terms of trade, Egon didn't doubt in the slightest that Ottó was the right person to conclude the deal. He made sure that Ottó had all the necessary comforts take care of so that he could concentrate exclusively on his mission. Plane tickets and hotel accommodation were arranged, and on top of that **he received a considerable**

amount of cash from his employer for any other travel expenses or expenditures he may happen to have.

Ottó liked travelling and so he looked forward to spending a couple of days in the luxurious environment of a Dutch hotel with all costs paid by the company while cashing in decent allowances. He was already knowledgeable about the company's products and knew what the ideal conditions of cooperation would be. His task was to negotiate them. He was excellent at the art of communication with customers and he believed that he would soon stupefy his new employer by achieving the desired result.

All plans thwarted

But, as ill luck would have it, poor Ottó got robbed immediately after arriving in the Netherlands. A dexterous pickpocket must have clung to him in the crowd of people leaving the airport gates and robbed him of everything he had in his breast pocket. Fortunately, Ottó wasn't robbed of his documents and payment cards that he kept in his briefcase. But unfortunately, what was stolen was an envelope in which he kept the cash from his employer. He had wanted to keep it close in a safe place, but a moment's lack of concentration meant that all the money was gone.

When Ottó noticed he had been pickpocketed in the taxi on his way to the hotel, he was shocked and thought about what to do. He didn't call the police, but he had the presence of mind to go to the Hungarian Embassy, where they issued **a confirmation for his employer** regarding the theft.

Egon was sorry about the lost money and also for the new employee. He expressed his sympathies to Ottó and promised that he would naturally reimburse all the costs that Ottó would have to pay using his own cash. Ottó certainly wasn't shy about spending money on his business partners as well as himself, and one could tell he was trying hard to leave an impression by spending ostentatiously. Whether it was thanks to this strategy, or some of his other abilities, he succeeded in negotiating the conditions requested by his employer, so he expected praise upon his arrival, **in addition to getting all his receipts paid**.

In the shadow of doubt

As one would expect, Egon was very happy because the new cooperation promised high future profits. Still, he couldn't fight off the bitter aftertaste of **the outrageously high costs of winning the business partner**. When checking the receipts Ottó presented him with, he shook his head in disbelief – not only at the total, but also their content. When he asked Ottó to explain why he bought luxury lingerie, Ottó claimed without blushing that it was a gift for a Dutch businesswoman who had slowed down the negotiations with her remarks and doubts. Egon didn't remember such a woman being part of the Dutch team, so he called the Netherlands to ask about how things actually were. It turned out that the meetings were held exclusively at their headquarters, which meant that Ottó had repeatedly **invited somebody else to the luxury restaurants** on the receipts.

Egon was cautious, so he decided to check the other facts he was given as well. When he called the embassy and asked to talk to the person who had signed the theft statement, he learnt that a man of that name actually worked there, but only as an auxiliary clerk who **was not authorized to issue such documents**.

A moment of carelessness

Egon had more and more doubts, so he decided to contact Ottó's former employers again to check whether they had happened to have similar experiences with him. The first number was unavailable, but the second call was answered by a surprisingly familiar voice. Ottó even introduced himself with his own name, as it didn't occur to him that he should have played the role of his well-satisfied former employer.

The course of events moved rather fast from there. As it turned out, Ottó hadn't left anything to chance and was **a real professional when it came to cheating**. Two of the phone numbers that he had provided as reference contacts belonged to him, the third was that of his best friend. It wasn't that hard to predict when the potential employer would check the references, so they had both introduced themselves with fake names and reeled off the complementary fable they had prepared.

It came out later on that Ottó really had fair-weather friends all around him. When Egon found contact details for his former employers on the Internet, he wasn't very surprised to learn that they, too, had had to cope with similar embezzlements, including very unfortunate situations in the Netherlands when this "luckless fellow" was robbed on almost every business trip he took. Of course, it was always confirmed by **a statement issued by the same clerk at the embassy**. No wonder, it was actually Ottó's cousin! They split the easy money and together enjoyed several days of luxury at others' expense. It was no surprise that Ottó candidly loved his travels to the Netherlands.

Unfortunately for him, he didn't get another chance to travel there for some time. In addition to immediately losing a lucrative job, just like his cousin, he went to court and later to prison, since the sums that he misappropriated in such a cunning way over the years were not negligible. Well, not all travellers' journeys have a happy ending.

What is the lesson to be learnt?

- When it comes to business trips, cheating is commonplace.
- A typical trick **when travelling by plane** is that the employer pays for a higher class, whereas the employee switches tickets and flies in a lower class, keeping the money reimbursed for the difference.
- The same practice occurs with **accommodation**.
- When it comes to money and **paying travel expenses**, I recommend being cautious and not giving your employees cash.
- **A company payment card** with a limit will keep you from worrying. What is more, you will know where your employee spent the money and what for. It will also make it easier for you to separate personal expenses from business ones.

Remember:

- Employees often cheat when reporting costs for business trips.
- Never give your employees cash when they go on a business trip, not even an advance payment for the business trip including allowances. It is always better to give them an insured payment card.

- Make sure the reported costs are real and that they haven't been adjusted. If your employees often go to the same place, it pays to have agreements with certain hotels and give them preference. That will also make it easier for you to assess whether the costs reported are appropriate.

- As for gifts and hospitality, it is a good idea to have rules for cost reimbursements defined in your internal regulations, for instance, what events and presents are unacceptable or to what amount your employees may cover your business partners' spending. Every employee should be reminded of such rules before each business trip, and you should check whether they have been adhered to.

The best friend

Although the employer in the previous story was rather vigilant, he was still taken in by a fraudulent employee with fake references. Is it actually possible to suffer even more damage in a similar case? Yes, it is.

You may fall victim to somebody who you never expected would string you along. A person who you didn't feel the need to check and whose CV statements you believed. Not because you are imprudent – on the contrary, you know such a person very well and don't need to ask anybody else because you have been through so much together!

However, there is a big difference between going out to have a few drinks with your best friend and giving him a job. Staking your life on somebody you haven't seen for many years could backfire on you.

Place: **USA**

Main characters:

Victim: Alan, company owner	×	**Employee:** Jim, financial manager

An encounter after many years

Alan and Jim had been friends since school and they had always got on very well. Their friendship continued even while they were at college, so they had shared a lot of experiences.

Together they went through their first loves at school, they shared study successes and failures, their joys and doubts, and they helped each other out of trouble resulting from the rashness of youth, just as best friends do.

After graduating from college, their paths parted. They stayed in touch for some time, but then Jim moved to another state where he had a partner and got a job and the friendship slowly fizzled out.

Meanwhile, Alan was building a successful company. Some years later, when Alan was searching for a new financial manager, as chance would have it, Jim was among those who showed up for an interview.

An informal interview

The job interview became a mere formality. Alan **remembered well** how reliable Jim was as a friend, that he was smart and never left him high and dry. Alan recalled all these positives about Jim when the old friends chatted, instead of conducting a proper interview, and he remembered the good old times as they swapped one story after another.

They both felt like soul mates again. As if the few years when they hadn't been in touch hadn't affected their friendship at all. Alan thought it was a good sign and felt that it was destiny that their paths had crossed again.

Who else could he entrust with his company finances if not his old friend? A friend who didn't have to prove anything, because what they once went through together was better than thousands of references. Alan didn't doubt for a second that Jim was right for the job, and he wasn't very interested in his employment history. After all, he knew best who he was dealing with.

Absolute trust

Jim tried hard from the very start to meet Alan's expectations. After a couple of months when he found his footing he became the only person who Alan trusted to communicate with suppliers, including issuing invoices and making payments.

Jim became cocky. When he didn't come to work every now and then, nobody checked on what he was doing. He had Alan's complete trust! It was kind of automatically assumed that he was at a business meeting. So it happened more and more often that he was unavailable. To do a job with such responsibility well is very time consuming!

Alan ignored the poisonous rumours that slowly spread throughout the company. Different sources mentioned more and more often that Jim was seen at bars and restaurants until the small hours, while **nobody happened to see him at work the following day**.

What eventually caught Alan's attention was news that seemed to be too far-fetched even for rumour, so he decided to check it. One of his employees who was found to be under the influence when reporting for a morning shift defended himself by saying that he couldn't leave the bar any sooner because Jim refused to let him go home and insisted he keep him company. What's more, he paid for everything, even for several other people. He **boasted they were drinking at the expense of the company** and invited everyone to have some more.

Shattered illusions

Alan went to that bar in person and he was not happy to find his friend there very intoxicated. Jim was so drunk that he didn't realize at first that it was his employer standing in front of him. He started to invite his old friend for a whisky – he had already had more than one by then.

Only then did Alan start taking more interest in what Jim had done during the time they hadn't seen each other. First, he was unpleasantly surprised to find out that his former classmate **had been through treatment for alcoholism twice, without success, and he even had a criminal record** because he had assaulted a waiter who dared to request that he pay a fat bill. Being an alcoholic, Jim was often broke, which was the case the night of his arrest, so instead of paying he beat up the waiter and ran away. He had been on probation ever since and couldn't find a good job. So running into Alan and getting employment from an old friend who didn't check his past was a small miracle for him.

Unfortunately, the combination of an expensive alcohol addiction and his employer's almost unlimited trust caused Jim to go too far. Alan couldn't believe how careless he had been after he discovered more and more details about what a good "business" his former friend made of the job. He didn't settle for just shirking work. His passion for night life ruined him very quickly, so he came up with what he believed to be an ingenious idea.

He started forging invoices and he changed the company bank account number on them to his private one. He did so every time he was short of cash and he also made sure the customer paid the invoice promptly.

Double loss

When Alan had his accounting audited in order to enumerate the damage suffered, he couldn't believe how insolent his friend had been. He must have known that it all would be revealed one day! However, alcoholics ignore possible consequences and only care about meeting their immediate needs. He must have been in agony in prison, where he ended up after Alan reported the embezzlement to the police because he was still on probation.

But Alan never heard anything about that. He didn't want to have anything to do with his ex-friend. He regretted losing a friend who he had completely trusted more than suffering a considerable financial loss. He was angry at himself for being so gullible and for realizing too late that people change and even best friends should be checked.

What is the lesson to be learnt?

- **Check your future employees!**

- This rule applies to **everyone without exception**. The fact that you were friends with somebody twenty years ago is no guarantee of a clean criminal record.

- Since you put your cards on the table when showing applicants what you have built and you're offering them a job opportunity, applicants should do the same by giving you their **references**.

- Don't let **nostalgia take over**. If your friends have made headway, they will certainly be happy to boast.

Remember:

- Be careful about employing good friends and relatives. Employment of family members usually fails to meet expectations on both sides. Relatives automatically expect above-standard treatment and think that you will turn a blind eye when assessing their work performance. And you may feel awkward refusing to play by their rules if you want to avoid bad blood in your family. Moreover, by tolerating such a situation you disadvantage other staff members who will eventually end up demotivated.

- So, before employing a friend or relative, consider whether it may cause you more harm than good.

- If you decide to employ a friend or relative, at least check them with the same diligence as you would other employees.

- Even in such cases you need to check their references, qualifications, diplomas and certificates.

IN CONCLUSION

There are companies that offer "screening", which means they check job applicants. It pays to use their services not only when hiring managers but also cleaners, for example, if they have – just like managers – access to sensitive data or information and other company assets or even money.

Sadly enough, two out of three employers expect that applicants exaggerate information about knowledge and responsibilities in their past jobs, so they often don't bother to check references, let alone check whether all the information is true. In fact, even these "white lies" should discourage employers from giving jobs to such dodgy applicants.

Chapter IV:

The showdown – face to face with a professional

If you've been duped by a job applicant's embellished CV, you are definitely not the only one. Among applicants there are oftentimes "professional cheaters" who stop at almost nothing. Some of them have enough guts to completely make up their education, regardless of the trouble they may cause by not doing their job properly, if they happen to get it.

For you as an employer, it can become a big problem. If your company is liable for certain decisions or steps you take as a legal entity, you are also responsible for selecting suitable employees who are eligible to perform the given tasks. For instance, if a judge forges his diploma and lies about his experience, who do you think will be held responsible for his rulings? In most cases, the people dissatisfied with the proceedings will sue the state, not the judge.

This chapter differs from the previous one in that you're going to read stories about incidents where cheating with CVs was very sophisticated and very difficult to reveal. You will probably remember hearing about some of these stories in the news, and reading through the following cases should convince you that one can never be careful enough and that it is absolutely necessary to verify things properly.

Following a dream

They say that if you really want something, you should try as hard as you can: follow your dream and don't get discouraged by anything or anyone. Some people take this too literally, and if they have been dreaming of a certain job, they may fail to see that not having the necessary qualifications or education is an obstacle.

For them the requirements in ads are nothing but clusters of letters, and they can be replied to accordingly with similar clusters. There's nothing easier than coming up with the right answer when you know the question. Then all you need to do is to look confident enough and hope that you get away with it. Only very few employers expect such immense impudence and brashness from applicants, and so they easily swallow the bait.

Place: **USA**

Main characters:

Victim: Sebastian, owner of an IT company	×	**Employee:** James, creative IT director

Innocent lies

As I have already mentioned, the fact that applicants tend to **embellish** the information in such an important document that decides – to a great degree – whether or not they get the job is, sadly, not only tolerated by a large proportion of HR managers and employers, but even kind of expected.

In most cases, they claim that their passive knowledge of a foreign language is fluent, they add some pieces of experience or skills here and there, they present themselves, despite their obligations, as absolutely flexible, all their hobbies relate to the field in which they wish to work and their weakness, if any, is "workaholism"!

Their efforts are encouraged by dozens of motivational articles available on the Internet that recommend exactly such an approach. If you want to succeed at a job interview, find out as much information as you can about the company and emphasize in your CV and covering letter exactly those aspects that fit the given profile.

Often, it is not a big lie. **An experienced HR manager is able to reveal the truth in such tales**: it usually sits somewhere half-way. And if you still have doubts, there's nothing easier than checking applicants' self-proclaimed knowledge and skills and asking them for certificates and other documents to confirm their education and capabilities.

Automatic prerequisite

Sebastian, the owner of an IT company, was one of those employers who came to realize during his years in business that education isn't everything. He was more concerned about the actual work each employee was able to do rather than how they looked on paper.

Nevertheless, when he was looking for an IT director, he insisted on some education. While he could hire clever young programmers who had gained experience programming at night at home, such an important management position required, among other things, the profound scope of general knowledge needed for leading and supervising a team of programmers.

So, during the interviews, he considered certain sections of the CVs presented as a mere formality and focused rather on each applicant's approach and interest in the job. He also assessed how they would fit in with the team. James seemed to be the perfect candidate in these respects, and his zeal made him stand out.

Two university degrees from a prestigious university and the confident conduct of an expert in computer science suggested he would become a great asset to the team. A duly defined probation period applied to James, just as to any other new employee, during which he got the chance to demonstrate what he could do.

Show us what you've got

James was duly proud of getting this dream job and threw himself headlong into his work. From the very start he was particularly friendly with all his colleagues, showed a sincere interest in their work and asked about their projects in great detail. He naturally commanded respect and everything seemed just fine.

At the end of his first week, just when James was flirting a bit with the HR manager, she recalled that she hadn't yet received copies of the certificates and university diplomas that he had referred to in his CV. The new IT director was at first taken aback a little, but without hesitation he promised to bring them soon.

The following couple of weeks he kept forgetting about them or said he couldn't find them, so the experienced HR manager one day finally waved her hand telling him not to worry about it anymore, since she – following Sebastian's instructions – had asked the university to send them copies.

A grouch with perfect attendance

From that time on, James was a changed man. He was shut up in his office all the time. He looked distracted and nervous and couldn't concentrate. He often raised his voice when talking to his inferiors and his natural command for respect was soon gone. They soon started to think of him as a lonely grouchy guy, and they didn't understand what had happened to the charismatic director he had once been.

There was one thing he excelled at: he was an incredible early bird, which was unique in the IT industry. The programmers were used to working at night and sleeping late in the morning. And although James could have arrived at work later than them, he was always among the first to show up in the morning.

James's probation period was going to end soon and Sebastian was still waiting for more noticeable results, but in vain. Since James had stopped spending time in the main room with the others and had started shutting himself up in his office instead, he wasn't able to accurately present what his team were working on, let alone what they had achieved in their projects.

Suspicion created by his own fear

Every time Sebastian stepped into his office, the first thing James did was switch off his screen, and he started confusedly flicking through papers on his desk. Naturally, this was extremely suspicious, so his employer decided to take a closer look at what James was actually doing at work.

It didn't take long for him to discover why James was arriving so early every morning. He wanted to **keep all the incoming mail under control** so that he could destroy the proof of his fraud: the letter from the university that would reveal that he had never studied there. He planned **to replace the letter with a forgery**.

Instead of waiting for his rendezvous with destiny, he spent time and company assets on making a perfect copy of the university letter including his faked diplomas. James was actually very skilful and creative when it came to making up such things. He believed that, if he persisted, he would eventually succeed in wriggling out of his lies. He had exerted so much effort to get this dream job!

He didn't realize that because he was spending so much time checking the mail and making counterfeits – and his absent-mindedness due to the permanent stress and fear of being revealed – **he was neglecting his work. Ironically, that was the reason why his boss focused on him more closely** and made a couple of calls to people who were listed in James's fabricated CV. No wonder it wasn't long before that dream job at Sebastian's IT company was available again.

What is the lesson to be learnt?

- Don't believe everything that applicants tell you about themselves, even if they present it in writing. **Check their references and education** before you hire them.

- Inclinations towards lying, manipulation and fraud as well as good qualities can be reliably revealed by well-compiled **psychological tests** that should be part of **job interviews**.

If you think something like this is unlikely to happen, I can give you several infamous examples of people with limitless insolence and excessive self-confidence whose CV embellishments were publicized in the media.

For instance, Jeffrey Archer, a writer and **former member of both chambers of the UK Parliament**, claimed for many years to have a diploma from Oxford University. Later it came to light that **he had merely declared himself to be an expert in English, geography and history**. A funny detail is that he added an impressive acronym to his name: FIFPC. Sadly for him, it came out later on that it was not a degree earned by university studies, but **the abbreviation of a body-building club**.

David Tovar wanted to become **the vice-president of corporate communication** for Walmart so badly that he faked details about his education in his CV. The US retail chain discovered David's lie when **considering him for a promotion, at which point they tried to verify the university degree** that David actually didn't have.

So that the list isn't solely made up of men, I'll also mention a woman who lied in her CV about her education. Alison Ryan, **a spokesperson for Manchester United**, claimed that she had graduated cum laude with a degree in history from Cambridge University. A woman whose task it was to take care of the club's PR actually caused its biggest PR faux pas when it came out that it was a lie and that she had been banned from another industry for cheating and circumventing rules.

Remember:

- In addition to checking the information in applicants' CVs, also check whether their diplomas don't happen to be just the work of a skilful graphic artist.
- Don't hesitate to use psychological tests as part of the selection process. They will help you reveal potential liars and cheaters. If someone proves to be untrustworthy once, you can never believe them again. If someone lies or fakes a document at the beginning, what do you think the chances are that they will do it again in a critical situation, for instance, when reporting results to qualify for annual bonuses? Do you believe that such people won't manipulate or "bend" figures in their favour?
- Invest enough time in finding out what your employee-to-be's actual skills are.

- When hiring employees for key positions, it pays to use an "assessment centre" consisting of games and tests taken over the course of several days that test applicants' capabilities when under pressure, whether they are good team players and the like. The results are assessed by experienced HR professionals and/or psychologists.

The job hopper

Job hopper is a term that is being used more and more when it comes to employment. What exactly is a job hopper? It may be someone who yearns for education, or it may just be an ordinary "professional" shirker. Whatever the case is, job hoppers are usually a hard pill for employers to swallow and employing them may result in vast losses. Well, judge for yourself.

Place: **Czech Republic**

Main characters:

Victim: Radomír, company owner	×	**Employee:** Vladislav, enthusiastic novice

Just what the doctor ordered

This story takes place in the Czech Republic, but it could have happened anywhere in the world. You're searching for a new employee, and you notice the CV of one applicant who has a history of repeated short-term employment. In fact, you can assume that there have been many more jobs, but the applicant only listed those that could prove useful during the job interview with you. Such people will probably argue that they didn't stay long at their previous jobs for numerous reasons, but they were never the ones to blame.

Job hoppers are usually people who are trying to "find themselves" and they won't settle for working just for money. They are searching for an occupation that they feel they could do for the rest of their lives, and they seem to be lucky enough to have found it in your company.

Know-it-all and Jack-of-all-trades

Vladislav was one of those know-it-alls who try many jobs but never stay for long. He had thousands of logical explanations as to why he had left his previous jobs, ranging from a bad atmosphere in the team to unsuitable working hours to a boss who didn't appreciate the demon for work he had in him.

Radomír, an owner of a private mechanic garage, couldn't be bothered to check Vladislav's arguments with his previous employers. He was okay with seeing that Vladislav was enormously interested in the job. His past didn't matter much to him. He needed a dexterous guy for the garage, and Vladislav was enthusiastic about the job.

Radomír appreciated that Vladislav seemed to be an easygoing fellow who could effortlessly arrange everything with customers, no matter how demanding they were. He was talkative and seemed to be a good worker. Who cared that he hadn't studied to be a car mechanic. He had determination to spare and **paying for some courses and training for a new employee is always a good investment**!

Vladislav didn't leave anyone in doubt that he would soon become an accomplished and enthusiastic car mechanic. So Radomír arranged all the necessary courses for him and looked forward to having a properly trained Vladislav in the garage working at full stretch.

An eager student

The first couple of months, Vladislav didn't see much "action". He attended all the courses and training sessions paid for by his employer and reassured Radomír that his investment would surely pay off. He **was an incredibly diligent student** who was beyond reproach. But when he was supposed to switch from theory to practice, everything suddenly changed.

He started suffering from odd sicknesses and other health issues, and instead of working, he spent a lot of time at doctors' offices undergoing various check-ups and tests. When he was required to do some work, he always had a lot of excuses and explanations as to why he couldn't do this or that. **It wasn't long before he handed in his notice**. He said he had discovered that it wasn't the job of his dreams after all and he had realized he wasn't suited to the role.

All the owner got out of paying for this "student" for several months was the opportunity to sponsor another experience he wasn't interested in. Radomír only regretted that he hadn't checked even one of the millions of reasons and arguments why Vladislav had never stayed in one job for long.

It is no fun to invest in the education and skills of your employees, expecting a return on your investment in the form of flawless work performance, and then end up finding out that a **freshly trained employee intends to run off**. In most cases, such "professional trainees" don't ever change their schemes – they simply move on to another company where they continue to improve their education at the expense of another employer.

Recently, there was a special survey on the employment fluctuation of young people under thirty-five that revealed that around 40 per cent of them are ready to change jobs immediately, and they are actually only waiting for a better opportunity. Moreover, they are often able to earn extra money thanks to the Internet, and they consider their freedom to be fundamental. This is also linked to settling down and having a family at a later age. The times when people got a job and hoped they would keep it until they retired are long gone, and one should take that into account when hiring new employees.

What is the lesson to be learnt?

- **Read CVs carefully** and don't just go with your first impression. Don't see it as a mere formality. Most people have the tendency to embellish many facts, but a cautious eye can reveal alarming information.
- **According to statistics, employers break even on new employees about a year after they are hired and trained**. If an employee leaves during that period, or shortly afterwards, your investment results in a loss.
- So, if you see in a CV that an applicant frequently **switches jobs**, you should certainly **be alert**. Unless such applicants have frequently changed jobs because of moving or health issues, or unless they work in a sphere where frequent rotation is expected (IT specialists, employees of shared-service centres, call centres and the like), you are probably looking at a professional job hopper. Any cooperation between you and such an employee will only be short-lived and you will be their sponsor.

Remember:

- In addition to looking at the other information in CVs, look at how often applicants have switched jobs, how the jobs are related and whether they have worked in the same or a similar industry.
- During interviews you should also focus on how interested the applicants are in the job you need to fill or whether they seem to care more about the benefits and training provided by your company.
- If you pay for expensive training for employees, have them sign an agreement stating that they have to work a certain number of months or years for you, otherwise you are entitled to a reimbursement of the costs of their training. In cases where employees working in more important positions could later misuse the information they get about your company or your clients, employ them on the condition that they sign a non-compete clause.

Doctor Janka

Medicine is one of the hardest professions to study for. No wonder: no matter what the specialization is, every doctor has the great opportunity to help patients as well as the immense responsibility for every single decision they make and operation they perform.

The amount of risk varies depending on the physician's specialization, but that doesn't mean that, for instance, a dentist cannot irreparably harm someone's health. It is a job intended only for seasoned professionals, and their education and experience play a crucial role.

Fortunately, medicine is a field that nobody would dare to engage in without relevant education and experience. Or would they?

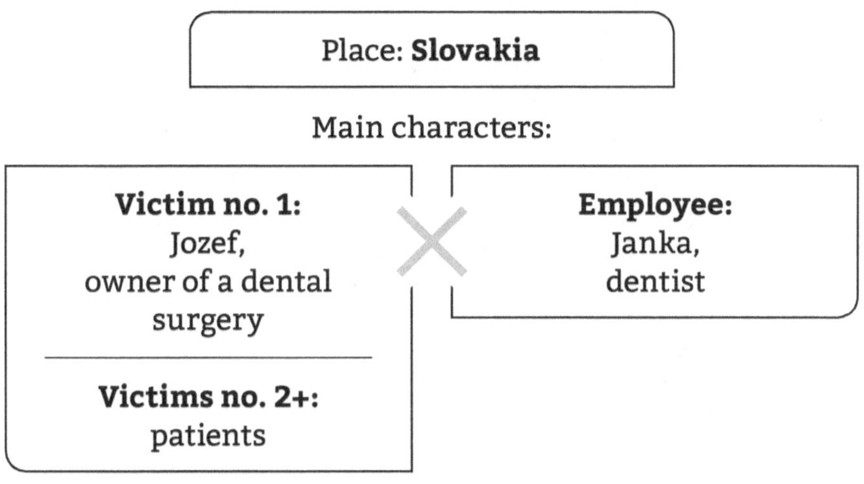

Making a childhood dream come true

Janka always knew what she wanted to be when she grew up – playing doctor was her favourite game. As the years passed, she became more and more attracted to dentistry.

At first, she didn't pass the university entry exams, but she was determined not to give up. Medicine is a prestigious field, so many students succeed on the second or third try. For the time being, she started working as a nurse in a dental surgery so that she could gain some experience before trying again to get her university degree. Such experience would certainly come in handy later on.

A newly established surgery

A couple of years later, Jozef, a dentist and entrepreneur in one, opened a new dental surgery. In addition to the staff that he brought along with him, he was looking for several new people to complete his team.

Janka used the opportunity, and at the interview **she was able to back up her brand new diploma with several years of experience from a dental surgery**. Jozef was delighted and he was happy to welcome her to his team. He found Janka nice, and she obviously knew what she was talking about. She did very well at the interview, and she wasn't reluctant to work long hours. Any employer would appreciate such enthusiasm from an employee.

Mutual satisfaction

The following nine years she treated patients, drilled their teeth, gave them fillings, wrote reports for health insurance and so on. Everything a dentist normally does.

It may happen to any doctor that patients come and go. Sometimes it is because they move house, sometimes there is a difference of opinions. The same happened to Janka a couple of times, however, the difference was that her former patients told their new dentists that they were surprised by **how different her procedures during the treatment were**.

Naturally, some questions and negative remarks from colleagues reached Jozef's ears, but he just considered them to be slander spread by the competition. Moreover, patients often cannot distinguish which procedure is appropriate in a specific case – it is up to the dentist to decide. But then a great shadow of doubt grew in him after one of his colleagues started working for another surgery where **several dentists who**

were supposedly Janka's university classmates worked. To his great surprise, none of his new colleagues knew her.

The fateful moment

That triggered a shocking revelation. Janka hadn't stop playing the doctor game despite becoming an adult, and she was still only a qualified nurse when she started working for Jozef. She had actually **considered his advert a challenge**. The fact that she didn't have the required education was no big obstacle to her – she had plenty of experience gained over all those years.

She sat down at her computer with an easy conscience and after several hours of fiddly work **she had conjured up a diploma** so impressive that even the university she supposedly graduated from wouldn't be ashamed of it. Well, at least she didn't lie about the fact that the diploma was brand new.

However, the incident had very troublesome consequences for Jozef and his surgery. Quite logically, **the health insurance company** concluded that for nine years it had paid for operations that were not performed by a qualified person, so **it claimed its money back**. Jozef had to work very hard to save his surgery from going under because of a childish game. If I leave aside the unexpected financial burden that he had to quickly cope with, there were still patients who lost confidence in his surgery. And it is very hard to regain lost or damaged confidence as you'll see in the stories that follow.

What is the lesson to be learnt?

- Although it may seem a bit far-fetched to you, this story actually happened. Not decades ago, but quite recently. As you can see, even if you think that you are ready for everything and that nobody can easily fool you like this, reality and the **capabilities of some employees can give you a very unpleasant surprise.**

- Jozef was and still is an educated and intelligent man. His big mistakes were **that he trusted people** and that **he relied on a good first impression and his instincts rather than reason and pragmatism**. Therefore, once again, I appeal to all those who are about to hire new employees, especially for important positions, to **verify their CVs and previous experience**. Making a few phone calls and asking for references may save you a lot of trouble.

Remember:

- ▶ You should check employees, especially those working in specialized fields such as lawyers, IT specialists and doctors, with utmost care, focusing on their professional approach, expertise and continual professional development.
- ▶ Don't be easily duped by good looks or the applicant's exceptional behaviour or personal charm.
- ▶ If you neglect the above stated recommendations, you may cause yourself considerable financial losses or any other kind of damage, and your company may suffer irreparable loss of customer loyalty and damage to reputation.

Frank Abagnale

I think I don't have to tell you who this man is – but this book would be incomplete without him. I probably cannot tell you anything new about him, since Frank Abagnale became world-famous after a successful film based on his real-life story was made.

However, he definitely belongs here, as he was **the most fraudulent employee of the millennium**. He embellished his CV with so many things that I can't think of anybody who could match him in this "discipline". But even though I look at his cons from the perspective of an employer, I still cannot fight back a certain feeling of liking for him.

This man has done a lot of stunning things, and for the sake of objectivity it should be said that **almost none of his employers complained about his work**. Of course, with the exception of the financial institutions who had a really hard time with him. As a forger, he was actually phenomenal.

Place: **USA**

Main characters:

Victims: lots of employers, clients and state-owned banks	×	**Employee:** Frank Abagnale, the world's most famous fraudster

A movie star

You probably know of Frank Abagnale thanks to Leonardo DiCaprio's perfect portrayal of him in the film *Catch Me If You Can*. Thanks to this film he has fans all over the world.

He must be given credit because, despite all his lies and fraud, he was very good at every job he had. And his forging skills eventually saved his neck. Thanks to the precision and perfection of his work as well as to his phenomenal knowledge of exactly how forging is done **he started cooperating closely with the FBI**. Today, **he is behind many protective elements** included in bank cheques and bills of exchange. At present, he is the head of Abagnale & Associates, a consultancy company focused on preventing and uncovering financial fraud.

Beginning a career at sixteen

It was forging cheques that started his "career". Although he was only sixteen at the time, he worked his way up very quickly and now is ranked as one of the most successful forgers of the twentieth century. Sixteen-year-old Frank took advantage of the fact that he looked older; so **the first thing he forged was his driving licence**, in which he made himself ten years older. He continued by adding several **fake identities** so that all his tricks weren't linked to his real name. He had a total of eight false identities that he used in connection with work. And there were many more names on his forged cheques.

Everything Frank did, he did with pleasure

Thanks to forged diplomas and certificates, he later **worked as a doctor, a pilot and an attorney**. He worked as a physician in the Paediatrics Department under the pseudonym of Frank Conners. Making the necessary documents to confirm his medical education was child's play for him. It was more difficult when it came down to the actual work. However, thanks to his charisma, he was able to work as a paediatrician for eleven months.

Frank Abagnale became a pilot for Pan Am Airlines after forging a pilot's licence and an airline employee ID card. At that time he used the name Frank Williams. During the two years he pretended to be a pilot, **he used various airlines to travel almost everywhere in the world for free**.

He was more responsible when it came to law (he actually successfully passed the bar exam), but he was still far from getting back on the right track. The entire time he had the police hard at his heels, but they were always left just a few steps behind. Frank was eventually caught in France, five years after his first con. During his time as a fraudster he had enjoyed an above-par life to the fullest and **cheated people in twenty-six countries**. All of those countries sought his extradition. After some rigmarole he ended up in the US, where he was later asked to work for the FBI, and so he soon started cooperating with them.

A writer with hands-on experience

Frank Abagnale **has written three books**. They were in extremely high demand and earned him over twenty million dollars. The movie *Catch Me If You Can*, filmed in 2000, was based on one of those books. In the other two books, *The Art of the Steal* and *Real U Guide to Identity Theft*, he focused **on the most common types of fraud and how they can be prevented and dealt with**. They are also good for those who wish two continue educating themselves after finishing this book.

What is the lesson to be learnt?

- Even though Frank Abagnale was unique, his story should serve as **a warning and a lesson** for all entrepreneurs and employers: you may come across – anytime and anywhere – professional liars and fraudsters who are willing to go to incredible lengths to achieve their goals

- Don't underestimate the options you have to hand, thanks to our modern times, that can help you reveal them before it is too late. Duly **check all applicants; contact their former employers** and ask them for recommendations, references or opinions; and be forthcoming when you are asked for the same by anybody else.

Remember:

- When it comes to harming employers, the inventiveness of some people has no bounds.
- Lies, theft, corruption and other kinds of fraud are some employees' daily bread, and sometimes even they don't realize they're doing anything wrong. There are cases where people buy a diploma just to achieve a certain goal or get a job that requires a certain qualification.
- Don't neglect your options to supervise them and reveal any illegal conduct.
- Use advanced IT tools and search social media. You might be surprised what information you find about your "perfect" candidate.

IN CONCLUSION

The more responsibility the job you need to fill requires, the more attention you should pay to checking applicants. Don't hesitate to verify all the data they present you with: naturally, you don't need to do it yourself. In addition to experienced HR managers, you can also make use of professionals who will do the checking for you. Our lives are influenced more and more by digitization, so you shouldn't hesitate to invest in IT systems or to dedicate some time to searching social media. Each of us leaves a digital footprint, and it is very easy to track down what we were actually doing at the times specified in our CVs.

And as I have mentioned: if you find that there is something inaccurate in the CV of a person that you want to hire for your team, take it as a warning sign. If the person lies and cheats before actually starting to work for you, how can you confide in such a person and delegate important tasks?

Chapter V:

Near is my shirt, but nearer is my skin – even a reliable employee may let you down

Based on the previous chapters, you may have come to think that risk is linked exclusively to new employees and that as long as you check them duly and everything proves to be alright, you can breathe a sigh of relief.

The truth is quite the contrary. According to statistics, ***up to 42 per cent of fraud*** *against employers is committed by people who* ***have been employed with them for between one and five years****. In fact, the probability of deliberate failure grows in jobs in upper management after five years of employment.*

That implies that you shouldn't take your eyes off those who have been working reliably for many years. The most common reasons for changes in their behaviour are ***personal problems of various kinds*** *– and if employees have a chance to improve their situation at work, they feel* ***safe*** *and sometimes they even think that* ***they are, in a way, entitled to it*** *after all those years.*

Micro-corruption agents

In this chapter, I would like to tell you something about micro-corruption. The term is a little unfortunate, as it may evoke images of bribery on a rather small scale.

In fact, it includes all kinds of manipulation and embezzlement of company money, including the manipulation of working hours or nifty rounding up of account balances. It is referred to as micro only because it is not macro and it is not corruption on a grand scale – for instance, in state administration – but it is misappropriation on a smaller scale that occurs inside a company.

The following story shows several of the faces micro-corruption may have in practice. Don't be fooled by the fact that the main characters in this story are women. The phenomenon of micro-corruption is also alive and well in the world of men, and, according to research, men can actually cause twice as much damage to their employers when compared with women.

Place: **Czech Republic**

Main characters:

Victim:
Leona,
company owner

Employee no. 1:
Jindřiška,
independent chief accountant

Employee no. 2:
Alena,
payroll accountant

A reliable right hand

Leona, a company owner, had hired Jindřiška as the chief accountant almost eight years ago, and there had never been a reason to complain about her. Jindřiška had always worked hard and had been precise, and with her work results and good approach, she had won Leona's trust and been given a lot of freedom.

At the time when the first discrepancies in company finances occurred, Jindřiška had been with the company for five years. Leona couldn't understand how **the company's costs kept rising** when she was trying so hard to achieve the opposite. Her negotiations with suppliers had been successful, but despite having lower purchase prices she still wasn't succeeding in cutting her costs.

Leona didn't doubt that the reports she was presented with were correct – the chief accountant printed all the accounting documents for her as usual and was ready to help should Leona have any questions. The results still showed excessive expenses in relation to suppliers and Leona started feeling desperate. The situation required an immediate solution in the form of decreasing orders and restriction to the assortment, but the owner's sixth sense told her there was something wrong.

A penny stolen is a penny earned

Her suspicion was soon confirmed when a supplier brought his own printout of payments to a meeting and they compared their figures. According to her records, Leona had paid twice as much for the deliveries as what the supplier had charged and actually received. The figures showed a difference amounting to almost 5,000 euros.

Leona thought there must have been a mistake in her accounting. It didn't cross her mind that it could have been done intentionally, but Jindřiška broke down immediately when confronted. She confessed that in the previous year **she had got into serious financial trouble**. If her family hadn't been threatened with the confiscation of their property as a result of her son's debts, she would have probably remained an honest accountant forever. At first, she had thought she could tell her employer about the problem and ask her for help, but she didn't have the courage to acknowledge such a big personal loss and put her good reputation at stake. She was afraid that she would lose Leona's confidence.

Instead of doing that, she found a way she could get the money to settle her son's debts without Leona noticing. All she needed was the implicit trust of her boss, which she – sadly for Leona – had. **So she forged some supplier invoices and charged them twice**. The only difference was that the original invoices were issued with the correct bank account number, whereas the illegal ones were modified to include her private account number. As she did all the transactions herself, the chances that she would get away with it were quite high.

She tried it once and **when nothing happened, she couldn't stop**. After some time, she got used to it and did it automatically. The pangs of conscience soon became routine. Nevertheless, the relief she felt from settling her son's debts was spoilt by mounting worries, that became certitude, that her double invoicing would be revealed one day. So, when it came to light, she actually felt relieved and confessed everything at once.

Alice in Embezzleland

It was a big shock for Leona. Of course, she sacked her chief accountant immediately, although she felt sorry for her on a personal level. But she couldn't trust her any longer. She then spent several weeks thoroughly checking her company accounting to find out how much damage she had incurred and what the final cost of Jindřiška's misappropriation would be.

She asked the payroll accountant to assist her: Alice was never exactly friends with Jindřiška, so Leona could expect that she would help her reveal the entire truth. But after she had been betrayed and become more vigilant, she couldn't get rid of the feeling that her payroll accountant didn't feel comfortable when she was around.

For a while Leona thought that she was being far too suspicious after her last experience, but she soon came across another surprise. She got a call from the manager of her Moravian branch to thank her for the meal vouchers that he had received for himself and his employees at the branch. He wanted to know whether he could promise his team that they would be getting meal vouchers regularly from then on.

At first, Leona didn't understand the question. She didn't know of any failure to deliver these employment benefits in the previous months; she wasn't informed of it. She was shocked to find out that the meal vouchers had actually only just arrived for the first time although the voucher programme had been introduced two years before!

As you may expect, the person who was responsible for sending them over was the payroll accountant. However, during all that time Alice had used – or more accurately misused – **the fact that nobody at the small branch of fifteen employees knew anything about the new benefit. She hadn't sent meal vouchers to any of them**. She kept them for herself and used them for her private shopping. Over the two years that she had this "side income", she earned over 10,000 euros on the vouchers that she "saved".

It may surprise you, but these two women, Jindřiška and Alice, didn't know about each other's embezzlement. And since each of them had a secret, they could never really become friends.

This experience led to a big disappointment for Leona, but also a lesson that she – as she later realized - needed. **You don't need to be overly friendly and trusting to be a successful and good employer**. I'm not saying that you should behave like a despotic tyrant. The best way forward is to gain natural respect and authority without evoking fear in your employees, while you can afford to be responsive without having to worry that your employees will misuse it. Being a successful person is hard. **Being a successful entrepreneur and employer is sometimes even harder**.

What is the lesson to be learnt?

- The **Association of Certified Fraud Examiners (ACFE)**, whose studies I deal with in a great detail at the end of this book, has issued a global study concerning micro-corruption. According to the study, the global impact of micro-corruption amounts to **5 per cent of company turnover**.

- **In Europe**, the result is even higher – **8 per cent**. That is over 20,000 euros a year in a medium-sized company.

Remember:

- Micro-corruption is a dangerous vice because it can be easily overlooked by employers.
- When fighting it, you need to use all the tools available, especially the most precise descriptions of all work processes, which must be constantly monitored and supervised.
- Make maximum use of your information system, even for employees who sit next to each other: this way, you will have control over their communication, work performed and projects.
- It pays to have employees rotate jobs at certain intervals. In cases where there is monotony and a lack of supervision, employees may start to feel that they cannot get caught. By having them switch roles, you can reveal these elements of micro-corruption and also start to improve the processes inside your company. Employee stereotypes actually cause blindness and passiveness when it comes to any changes or improvements.

A desperate mother

The following story involves a woman disappointing her employer, who had absolute confidence in her after she had worked for him for many years. She let her boss down in a way that is thought to be rather more typical of men.

As in the previous story about Jindřiška, there is another very powerful factor that is very hard to fight back: maternal instinct. Even in the animal kingdom, mothers are the most dangerous enemy you can come across, and their need to protect their babies can overshadow any other needs. And since the skin is closer than the shirt, employers have little chance of winning this game.

Place: **Hungary**

Main characters:

Victim no. 1: Izidor, owner of a betting company **Victims no. 2+:** betters and clients	×	**Employee:** Zita, an agile teller

He would bet on her

When Izidor was opening his betting office, he chose his employees carefully: only nice and reliable ones with clean criminal records. Zita started working for him the very first week, and after many years of working together they became friends. Her work performance was always flawless. Zita had Izidor's complete trust. They went through all kinds of things over those years, and she had always proved to be worthy of his trust.

Simply out, Izidor could always rely on Zita, and he couldn't imagine how his betting office would run without her. He was certain that whatever happened, even if the whole world turned its back against him, Zita would never let him down.

When the home fires stop burning

Zita, her husband and their small son weren't exactly well off, but they weren't suffering any hardships either. They lived in a new house in a small village not far from the capital. Just as many other people around them, they had a mortgage and they had to work hard in order to be able to make the payments while maintaining their standard of living. And they were able to do that for quite a long time.

Things changed when Zita's husband found a lover and the affair came to light shortly thereafter. However, he decided not to move out, although he felt like part of another household and thought that the duties related to the former one didn't concern him any longer. He used his earnings exclusively to pay for his new life, and he neglected the mortgage and his family.

Zita had to get used to being on her own with just her son, despite living with a suddenly estranged man who was still her husband. However, she wasn't able to pay all the bills and the mortgage. The trouble started the day she received a letter threatening repossession. She was totally without hope. Worries about her and her son's future took over. And a desperate mother is capable of anything.

Desperate people do desperate things

She couldn't explain why she went to a casino, sat down at a slot machine and threw in the first coins. When she realized three hours later that she had lost everything she had on her, she felt faint. She had done the worst thing she possibly could have. However, that night she came up with an idea how she could "save" the situation. She would borrow some money from work, win the lost money back, and then return it to the cash register.

From then on, things started to go very badly. Every day she sat at the betting office counter as she had done for many years before. And every day she took **cash that wasn't hers**. She always put aside some money and took it with her to the casino to feed the slot machines. Sometimes she did win a modest amount, but more often she left empty handed, feeling desperate.

Naturally, it couldn't go on like this forever and Izidor noticed that the money was missing. At first, he suspected everyone except Zita. She would have never stolen from him. Eventually, both of them were disillusioned. The loss incurred over several weeks amounted to three million forints.

What is the lesson to be learnt?

- We've come to the **must of having good safety measures in place** as we have a thousand times before and still will a thousand times more. This necessity is doubly important when your employees deal with cash.

- Another lesson to be learnt from this story: **even the best employees can go astray and become dangerous.** Their problems, not exclusively of a private nature, may completely change their nature and priorities.

- What this implies is that you should never **gloss over any warning signs**. Listen to your employees and be observant so that you **notice any changes** in time. If you can come up with a helpful offer to help solve their problem, you may be protecting your assets at the same time. Desperate people do desperate things, even though they may have never been prone to theft.

Remember:

- If your employees work with money, you must be vigilant and monitor the entire route of the cash through your company. Try to do without cash payments whenever possible. Instead, buy automated machines that receive money and print receipts.
- Carefully select the employees who will have access to money and pay enough attention to them once you hire them – ask about their family and health. Do random checks on a regular basis and consider using mystery shoppers.
- Never forget to conclude a material liability agreement with employees who work with money. It is absolutely necessary to have insurance that covers employee mistakes such as receiving counterfeit banknotes, coming up a bit short and the like.

Working his way up to prison

The following story is another example confirming that even originally good and loyal employees can become troublemakers, especially when things suddenly start going downhill in their personal lives. Destiny followed this storyline when it was writing the screenplay for the main character of this plot, with the difference that much higher cards were dealt.

When employees get into such serious trouble that they start breaking rules, they usually get caught in a vicious circle that is not easy to get out of. At such times, one thing matters more than anything else: how much power they have in their hands, meaning how much authority and freedom they were given by the employer.

Place: **Germany**

Main characters:

Victim no. 1: a bank **Victims no. 2+:** clients	**Employee:** Thomas, a very personal banker

The epitome of a successful person

Thomas started working for the bank as an ordinary teller. This shy boy soon worked his way up and became a cashier. His performance was so good that after several years he was offered a position as a personal banker. He fared very well in all of these jobs.

Being a long-time employee, Thomas had the complete confidence of his managers as he always took care of his VIP clients in accordance with his high standards and he seemed to be **an ideal and loyal employee** in every respect.

First doubts

However, one day a dissatisfied client contacted the bank claiming she was surprised to find out that a rather large sum of money was missing from her fixed-term account. The bank duly inspected her complaint and their findings were unpleasant. A total of almost 13,000 euros had been – via several transactions – transferred inexplicably from the client's account.

Her personal banker was Thomas, and he was logically the one to be assigned the task of finding out what had happened. However, he wasn't able to present any conclusive explanations, so the bank management came down on him and checked his accounts as well as the accounts of his other clients. The bank's suspicion that more clients could have been harmed grew when they found more and more inconsistencies, so they contacted the police.

The investigation revealed that the accounts of several other clients had also been charged with irregular payments and that all the money had been transferred to an account abroad from which it travelled through several other accounts until it got back to Germany, to the same bank. The account owner looked surprised when the police lashed out at him. He claimed that the money was sent by a friend who was getting divorced and didn't want to share the money with his ex-wife-to-be in the divorce proceedings.

Despair leads to failure

It soon came out that the friend who regularly withdrew cash from his account was Thomas. It was true that he was getting divorced and that his wife had a good reason for divorcing him. Her husband had **been a gambler** for many years.

As he kept losing more and more money, he felt more and more miserable and tried to drown his sorrows in spirits. The result was that he also **became an alcoholic**. By that time, he owed money to all his relatives as well as to many friends and neighbours. Thomas' wife couldn't stand it any longer, so she brought things to a close by filing for a divorce.

Thomas had figured out a way to get the money to feed his hungry addictions long before that. A lot of it was lying idly in the bank and often for no reason! Since he had **access to his relatives' accounts, he started by stealing small sums from them**.

When they started wondering where their money was disappearing to, Thomas had to extend his "clientele" and he started "borrowing" from people he didn't know. He focused on rich ones, who he presumed might not notice when small amounts were deducted from their accounts. Who knows, maybe if he had not stopped controlling himself in terms of the sums, it may have taken much longer before the first victim revealed the scam and required the bank to perform an investigation. Still, he got away with it for an incredibly long time before he was caught.

A five-year experience

When the investigation was over, the bank management couldn't believe it when they discovered that this had been going on for five years and that Thomas had caused them financial damage of 300,000 euros. This amazingly high sum was spent on gambling and alcohol. Do you think that is impossible? Well, it's a true story.

In fact, this case is not as unusual as one might think. Certain variations on this theme have happened and definitely keep happening in many parts of the world. And it is not so hard to guess where the main characters usually end up. In prison.

What is the lesson to be learnt?

- **Personal problems** shift the limits of honesty, even in the best people. Don't overlook **warning signs** that you notice in your employees.

- Research has shown that **65 per cent of typical offenders** in similar cases are men between the ages of forty-one and forty-five, usually with a university degree, who have been with the company between one and five years. When the fraud concerns someone in a senior management or leadership position, 65 per cent of such male offenders are between fifty-one and fifty-five years of age and have been with the company for more than ten years.

- Of course, I don't mean to say that all your employees who fit this profile should be **automatically suspected of crime**. But I feel it is my duty to draw your attention to these statistics.

Remember:

▶ In the cases of employees working with money, you should pay extra attention to their family matters, hobbies and any mental health or other health issues they may have.

- Adverse changes in their families or health may trigger the justification of stealing.
- There are high-risk groups with an increased probability of stealing your money.
- Introduce control mechanisms and define rules for approving money transfers and handling money that include at least two levels of approval. Ideally, the people working on these two levels don't know each other and aren't colleagues or friends.

Such a nice lady

An error can occur anywhere at any time, sometimes due to obsolete technology. Even the latest software may contain bugs, but it is developed with the intention of correcting imperfections in the previous versions, and it pays to invest in the latest updated versions.

Nevertheless, behind every machine and programme there is still a person who uses or operates it. And there is a thin line between use and misuse. The more sophisticated the bug a user who might be dealing with personal issues discovers, the longer such a person can successfully keep a newly established "small business" a secret.

Place: **Slovakia**

Main characters:

Victim no. 1: owners of a big company **Victims no. 2+:** some of the staff	×	**Employee:** Mária, an apt accountant

A low-profile long-term worker

Mária had been working as an accountant for a certain big company for twelve years. She was in charge of payroll for hundreds of employees, and she did her job very well, working entirely on her own. She had been an accountant her whole career, more than 40 years. During all that time she had continuously improved her education, so she was always aware of the latest amendments and currently valid legislation. Whenever anybody needed to know anything, they asked her and she always knew the answer.

She was a real treasure to her employers. She could have retired, but she didn't want to. She didn't have any children or grandchildren and, since she had become a widow, she had been living on her own. As she said, she had nowhere to hurry off to. Mária was rather reclusive. Over all those years she had never really become friends with any of her colleagues. It seemed as if she were avoiding them. She didn't go to company parties or any other events with colleagues. Everyone saw her as **an introvert and a lone wolf, but nice**.

People at work regarded her almost as fixed inventory, someone who could always be found in her office. One could say that it was the place where she felt most comfortable and safe. She never took days off, not to mention longer holidays.

Overpayments can sometimes be undesirable

When the social security office came to do an inspection because there was an overpayment on employment insurance, it seemed to be some sort of misunderstanding at first, and for a while the employers thought that they might get some money back. But when the HR manager and the inspectors compared their lists of the employees who the insurance was supposed to be paid to, they came across some names that shouldn't have been there.

The logical explanation was that Mária had simply omitted the fact that two servicemen were dismissed from the company several months earlier and hadn't stopped making their insurance payments. It was unclear how the payroll accountant could have calculated the exact amount, but Mária promptly explained it by claiming that she must have forgotten to cancel the standing orders in the accounting system.

If the state inspectors hadn't been so insistent, she would have got away with it. But, in the following hours, those stubborn clerks discovered another seven suspicious names that appeared in their list. They did not sound familiar to the HR manager either, so all the questioning looks were directed at Mária again, and she just shrugged her shoulders.

A good old soul

The employers were not far from feeling sorry for that sneaky lady, but a thorough check revealed why she had been so hardworking in the past and never left her office: she was afraid that someone might discover her **private pension fund**.

When her husband died some years before, she realized that her retirement was approaching and she started to worry about her future. When she had a job, she could afford to pay the rent for the spacious flat in which she had lived all her life with her husband, but she knew that when she retired her pension wouldn't be enough. She didn't want to move to another place, so she needed to find a way to make some extra money. Then she realized that she had the perfect tool in her hands: her company's accounting software.

Despite the size of the company, her employers were reluctant to **invest in new sophisticated accounting software**, and they were very happy that Mária was so skilful that she could make do with the old imperfect system. That simple programme was not linked to any databases, and all the data had to be typed in manually. There were no control mechanisms that would check any double payments or other errors. That was the accountant's job. But Mária never complained about the needless labour. She happily entered the employee and customer data manually.

Mária's fictitious employees

The software's weakness, which she took advantage of, was that it allowed her to add fictitious employees to the list. As you probably know, these were employees who may have never worked for the company and they certainly shouldn't have been in the database. In the course of four years, Mária transferred approximately 400,000 euros to various private accounts to stock up for her retirement, as **each month she transferred salaries to some twenty fictitious employees**. In order to eliminate suspicion, she regularly changed their names.

The programme is to blame!

When this fraud was discovered, Mária tried to persuade everyone that it all must have been just **some kind of error in the accounting programme**. As it couldn't match payments or print overviews, all the calculations were done by hand, and she insisted fiercely that it was just a mathematical error and a more sophisticated programme would have certainly pointed out the inconsistencies.

However, her bank account balances were clear evidence that it was no misunderstanding or blunder.

What is the lesson to be learnt?

- Mária used or – to be more precise – **misused the flaws and imperfections of obsolete software**. This clearly shows how important it is to make sure that you have **flawless technology in place** and that you don't let anyone manipulate your data or circumvent facts.

- Your information technology should be set up in such a way to **protect your system against any attacks from the outside as well as any violations on the part of your employees**. Ideally, there should be financial thresholds set, preferably via predefined approval processes; meaning certain tasks should be approved by more than one employee, while transfers of larger sums should be approved by the management or owner.

- Such preventive measures are essential, but you shouldn't imagine that everything will work automatically without your involvement. I recommend that you **monitor and check the system** every now and then, making sure it is still suitable. **Don't hesitate to update and upgrade it** whenever needed.

- At the same time, I must repeat what I've written before about high-risk employees. **Some signs of fraud** and dishonest behaviour can often be when **employees work too hard**, don't want to take days off, don't want to share their duties and **isolate themselves**. Naturally, there are exceptions, such as introvert workaholics, but you should still be attentive to such signs and never overlook them.

Remember:

- ▶ Continually update your information system so that your employees cannot find errors and gaps in it that they can misuse.
- ▶ Protect your internal information system against intruders from the outside and from the inside.
- ▶ Introduce approval processes that will ensure that responsibility is distributed among several people in your company and does not rest on a single employee.
- ▶ An overly hardworking employee who tries to take over the tasks of other colleagues may be a risk factor when handling money or other assets.

IN CONCLUSION

As I mentioned at the beginning of this chapter and you can see in the stories, you cannot rely on even the best employees unless you supervise and control them constantly, especially when you don't know what they are going through in their personal lives.

It is necessary to have effective control mechanisms in place, monitor your employees on a regular basis and communicate with them. What have proved to be useful are annual motivational interviews as well as psychological tests that may warn you in time about a change in an employee's behaviour or the occurrence of warning signs.

Chapter VI:

Like two peas in a pod – creative forgery

The stories in the previous chapter have illustrated several occasions where employees exerted incredible creativity when it came to forging documents.

Frank Abagnale, the king of forgery, will probably remain on his imaginary throne for a long time, but let's have a look at a few cases where some employees tried to dethrone Frank. What else are people tempted to forge, besides university diplomas, and what unusual things may be misappropriated with the help of forgery?

A fashionable part timer

Some jobs don't require permanent employees, so it's better to use part-time workers. That allows employers to quickly modify the number of employees according to current market demand following seasonal oscillations or to react efficiently to customer shopping behaviour.

Moreover, by offering part-time jobs you do society a good deed, as you give students an opportunity to earn some money while studying, among others. There are always lots of people interested in part-time work and it is not easy to choose the best candidate.

You will be happier if some of them prove to be good workers and you are able to establish a long-lasting cooperation. Such people may later even become full-time employees, as was the case for the owner of the fashion boutique in the following story.

Place: **Austria**

Main characters:

Victim: Harald, company owner	×	**Employee:** Gabriela, part-time worker

Making the best impression

Harald didn't need another full-time employee for his fashion boutique. He wanted a helping hand for weekends and for days when demand was higher. He was searching for somebody, preferably a girl, who was familiar with fashion, had a strongly customer-oriented approach and would be able to settle customer complaints with a smile on her face.

Gabriela, who applied for the job, seemed to be the perfect choice. A typical nineteen-year-old student who liked to look good and loved clothes, accessories and parties always needed some extra euros. She was attractive, kind and all smiles; she spoke in a refined manner and dressed tastefully.

Harald didn't doubt for a second that this nice, communicative and flexible girl would be more suitable for his shop than the retirement-aged woman who also applied for the job. His intuition told him that an up-and-coming, pretty young woman would sell more than a rather staid older lady, even though she had extensive work experience.

The perfect boost

Gabriela moved around the fashion world of the shop with innate grace. She soon knew everything about the assortment of goods they were selling, followed the latest trends, learnt to handle orders and to use the cash register. None of the customers at the luxury boutique ever complained about her.

On the contrary, everyone was very happy with the how obligingly she dealt with their complaints, if they had any. Gabriela was nice to customers, and she tried to accommodate the requirements of every person who came in to return goods. She didn't care much about their reasons for returning an item. She took back the goods, gave the customer a gift card for the relevant amount and wished them a nice day. A perfect approach to complaints, Harald thought.

He didn't like the stereotypical complaint procedure much, as it meant that every returned item decreased his profit. That's why he came up with the idea of exchanging goods for gift cards. His regular customers knew that when they came in to return something, they couldn't ask for their money back. They could choose between exchanging it for goods of the same price or a gift card for the value of the returned item. Most of them preferred gift cards.

Empty storeroom, full flat

After several months, Harald's accountant warned him of some discrepancies in his stock management. There were far too many items being returned without any apparent reason and the value of "purchases" made through gift cards was significantly affecting the shop's profit.

Harald wanted to ask Gabriela about the most common reasons why customers returned goods, but she appeared to be speaking on the phone, covering her mouth with her hand. It awoke curiosity and suspicion in him, so he decided to stay in the storeroom until the end of the working day. He saw, with his own eyes, Gabriela – unaware that she wasn't alone at work – selecting a few nice items of clothing and putting them in her bag. When he heard her pay with the beep of a gift card at the cash register, it all dawned on him.

Harald called the police immediately, and they went to search Gabriela's flat, which she had recently started renting because she didn't want to live in the university halls of residence anymore for some reason. The reason for her move soon became apparent: her flat was crammed full of clothes, shoes and accessories from the shop to the point where it resembled a warehouse.

Young, but skilful

Gabriela was really a skilful girl. A bit too smart and inventive for a nineteen-year-old. Who would have thought that she would be the one to **come across the flaw in the company computer system and would manage to make copies of gift cards**? So she had enjoyed above-par benefits for several months: she always issued a gift card for every item returned, uploaded the relevant amount on it and then she did the same with a copy.

Then she used the copy to "shop" for herself and her friends, and she even started selling the stolen goods on the Internet. Everything was still intact, with the tags from the shop, and it cost less than in a brick-and-mortar shop, so the goods sold well. Online customers often wrote to Gabriela asking whether she happened to have this or that, or if she had something in a different size. Gabriela was always happy to meet their requirements. "Restocking" was no problem for her.

This enterprising part-time worker cost Harald almost 20,000 euros in damage, and Harald was relieved to be able to fill the position with the experienced older applicant who had been his second choice before.

What is the lesson to be learnt?

- There are obviously fields where **visually representative employees** are required, although no one says it aloud for various reasons (the main one being that the employers don't want to risk being accused of discrimination).
- Many companies have internal dress codes regulating employee clothes, appearance and hairstyles. Nobody questions the rules stipulating that flight attendants have to fix their hair in place, doctors in an operating theatre must wear a mask at all times, bankers cannot meet clients wearing a T-shirt or shorts and construction workers are required to wear clothes that comply with safety regulations.
- Still, I don't recommend that you choose your future employees with your eyes only. Anyone can achieve a neat appearance. But a lovely face won't make up for a lack of loyalty, reliability and experience.

Remember:

- ▶ Be extra cautious when choosing part-time workers: they usually work for you for only a short period of time, and thus they are not motivated by career growth. You can always pair part-time workers with somebody else from your company who will mentor or supervise them, thus having their performance thoroughly checked.
- ▶ You should conclude material liability agreements with workers, even if you don't expect them to stay long.
- ▶ Pay increased attention to their behaviour and work performance – don't underestimate the value of regular checks.

Partying in style

Combining work with an eccentric personality may be complicated for some people, while others are surprisingly good at it, although often at the expense of their employers. If necessary, they pull a few tricks out of their hats to help them achieve their goals.

Stuart, the founder of a charity, could tell you some stories about that, particularly about his long-term employee Bart, from whom he didn't expect anything bad after many years of reliable work.

Place: **USA**

Main characters:

Victim: Stuart, the owner and founder of a charity	×	**Employee:** Bart, a very sociable senior manager

A timid sponsor and a meritorious hard worker

Stuart had always had a strong sense of social solidarity, so running a charity was a logical career option for him. He didn't expect sky-high profits from his business: on the contrary, he tried to help wherever it was really needed. He invested a lot of money in his organization at the start, and later on his main task was to get sponsors and other generous donors.

Bart, a fifty-year-old man, had worked for him for twenty years, half of that time as a senior manager. Stuart was happy to have such a good and hardworking organizer by his side. Bart was very well aware of the objectives and mission of the organization, and he independently searched for suitable projects that they could fund as well as for rich business donors.

An indispensable part of the organization's agenda was their participation in various charitable events and parties. Being an introvert, Stuart found them rather stressful. He didn't feel the need to be publicly visible, so he and Bart made a great pair, as Bart represented the company well at such events and with pleasure.

A media case like no other

When leafing through a regional newspaper, Stuart was shocked to come across a very critical article questioning the operations of his charity. The general public's confidence in charities was weak at the time, so journalists were focusing on fundraising projects and trying to find out whether the funds raised really got to where the organizers claimed.

Stuart thought that the misunderstanding would soon be explained and hoped that the article would not harm his organization's good reputation much. "Rumour has it" is half-truth, so he expected that some people would believe the article even if it were proved wrong. He needed irrefutable evidence that all the funds raised at their events were used for charitable purposes, so he asked Bart to prepare the necessary supporting documents for a spur-of-the-moment press conference.

Paralyzed and empty handed

However, instead of helping him resolve the situation, the senior manager made a U-turn: first, Bart said he had to leave the office unexpectedly to arrange something urgent at home, and then he switched off his mobile and was out of reach. When Stuart started inspecting the relevant documents himself, he broke out in a cold sweat as he soon realized the reason for his long-standing employee's disappearance.

It came out that with the exception of a few events that were really beneficial – by which Bart probably wanted to excuse his other actions – Bart had been sending "charitable contributions" to projects that had very little in common with charities. However, he had received fat provisions for intermediating generous grants and his personal remuneration was the only criterion he considered when distributing the money originally intended for good purposes.

In addition to that, he had had friends issue him false invoices every now and then – for instance, for cleaning services, holding social events and renting halls and buildings where various charitable events were supposed to have been held. Instead of charitable events, he had organized lavish private parties there.

At the same time, he awarded himself not exactly modest bonuses, probably to compensate himself more appropriately for the drudgery of the job than the salary Stuart paid him. If his boss intended to dedicate all his efforts exclusively to praiseworthy activities and supporting other people, that was his decision, but Bart was certainly able to take care of himself.

Losing a manager and a good name

Stuart had to cancel the press conference and launch an international manhunt for his employee. Due to the amount of damage caused over the years and the prospect of many years in jail, Bart packed his bags and disappeared abroad as soon as his actions came to light.

However, he wasn't afraid to take with him not just a company phone and laptop, but also –rather stupidly – a car with wrap advertising, which helped the police to find him. In a car chase like something from a Hollywood action movie, he hit a tree and was happy to get away (at least for the time being) with just broken ribs and a severe concussion.

Stuart lost much more than the car and money. He lost his faith and confidence in people. Rectifying the damage caused by his protégé in the field of charity was an almost impossible job

What is the lesson to be learnt?

- The infamous main character of this story is a typical example according to global statistics. Research shows that **embezzlement** within companies **is most often committed by men in middle and top management positions, aged forty-six to fifty-five**.

- While in most of Europe this age category leads, the situation is different on other continents where the age of fraudsters is lower. Some studies even mention men of about thirty-six years of age. The biggest motivation, as one would expect when it comes to asset misappropriation, is **financial benefit**.

- An interesting fact is that only **a negligible percentage of women** commit embezzlement.

Remember:

- If you decide to be philanthropic and you deal with other sponsors, never leave it up to your employees.
- If you let your employees make decisions about allotting money to charitable projects, you should always have the last word after checking everything thoroughly and considering all possible collisions with tax laws in the country where your business is and the like.
- Fund projects gradually, make them define their objectives and release further funds only after partial milestones are met. Check the progress of each project consistently and in detail.
- It is a good idea to donate material things or services rather than providing money. Misappropriating money is always much easier.

Cashing in on last hope

Whatever such crooks forge and whatever their intentions are, if they rob their employers, it is inexcusable and, in addition to getting sacked, such people deserve to be thrown in prison. If the damage is "only" monetary, as in Stuart's case, the situation can be rectified, although many problems need to be overcome.

But imagine the morals of the human hyenas who stop at nothing and don't mind deceiving helpless people when they are drowning and ready to grasp at any straw. For instance, when they or a close relative fall seriously ill.

Place: **Spain**

Main characters:

Victim no. 1: a university **Victim no. 2:** a research foundation **Victims no. 3+:** patients and their relatives	**Employees:** two professors, a civil servant and two laboratory research workers

Hoping for a miracle

Cancer is still one of the diseases that cannot be reliably cured. Research scientists all over the world have been trying to figure out how to beat it for decades. Sometimes it seems that a miraculous cure or treatment has been discovered, but it has never worked in all cases, and so mankind is still waiting for the right solution.

Meanwhile, patients are dying and, in their desperation, they try all sorts of things, from increased consumption of broccoli and shark cartilage to biological treatments linked with many side effects. Besides radiation and chemotherapy, which cannot be used effectively in all cases, conventional medicine doesn't leave them with many options. Consequently, they resort to various charlatans and, in better cases, to research teams who think they are on the right track to finding a cure that, having been tested on animals, now has to be tested on people. A hopeless patient often agrees to anything that offers at least a glimmer of hope. Otherwise, they're left with nothing but a vision of approaching death.

A foundation offering hope

Not long ago, many patients in Spain had cause to rejoice. There was a non-profit foundation under the patronage of a famous university and a research laboratory that was offering oncologic patients a certain miraculous preparation with convincing arguments about its guaranteed effects.

This foundation asked the patients and their relatives, who were willing to pay literally anything for the prospect of recovery, for an official contribution to their further research. Although we say that health is priceless, when a person has only one option it becomes a saleable commodity sold for a specific price. Naturally, there were many people who paid and underwent the treatment.

A painful awakening

After some time, the university was contacted by dissatisfied parents who had donated a huge sum to the foundation for several months of treatment for their daughter. Sadly, the girl passed away, and there were no signs that her condition had improved at all throughout the treatment. The desperate parents asked the university for an explanation, since the miraculous preparation hadn't improved their daughter's health as they had been promised.

The university management didn't understand the question at first, so they decided to look into the situation more closely. Soon they filed two criminal complaints against two of their professors and three external accomplices: two members of the research laboratory and an employee working for the state administration.

The university and the laboratory actually had nothing to do with the project. **Their names were misused to make the foundation look more trustworthy.** Its members had administered to desperate people a drug that hadn't received the necessary approvals from the pharmaceutical authorities for one simple reason: according to their findings, it didn't contain any active substances. And the people from the foundation were aware of that.

The investigation revealed that these five sly people, without a single drop of compassion in their hearts, had received at least 600,000 euros from gullible customers for this ineffective placebo. The cheaters had found their business of capitalizing on human hope very lucrative and had intended to expand their "portfolio" to include another supposedly miraculous, but in fact ineffective, cure for Alzheimer's disease.

What is the lesson to be learnt?

- If dishonest employees are determined to improve their situation, they won't be put off by anything. As soon as their consciences come to terms with breaking the rules, trespassing further imaginary boundaries becomes easier. For you, the employer, this should imply that even seemingly small swindles may lead to massive fraud that can badly damage your company. **Once a cheater = always a cheater**.

- With respect to your company's security, you should define your internal rules in such a way that you (meaning your company as a legal entity) are not held liable for any employee failures or criminal conduct. It is your employees who are to be held responsible for their conduct. You should have sophisticated **documents in place such as statutes, work rules and a code of ethics, and require all your employees to sign a confirmation stating that they have read and understood them**. Every employee must also be aware of the sanctions that may be imposed on them in case of a breach.

Remember:

- Some employees, when they get the opportunity, stop at nothing, not even at exploiting and increasing some one's misfortune.
- You should check the Internet every now and then to make sure that none of your employees are misusing your company's good name (in this case, it was a university's name) and getting rich at your expense.
- For a moderate fee, you can hire a specialized company that will monitor the news and information published about your company on the Internet.
- Hire a good lawyer to protect your company's good name if your employees misuse it.

Do you happen to be missing a freight container?

As the title of this story suggests, **anything can be stolen, even something highly visible** like a railway freight container full of goods. This rather peculiar case actually happened in Romania a couple of years ago.

I have included this story in the chapter about counterfeits, although the crime committed was typical embezzlement. Notice what some sticky-fingered employees are able to forge and do in order to "earn" some extra money. Ironically, although these thieves were extremely creative, their attempt failed because of their stupidity.

Place: **Romania**

Main characters:

Victims:
company owners

Employee no. 1:
production manager

Employee no. 2:
dispatch manager

An unclaimed freight car

Do you happen to be missing anything? This sentence began the following story. The owners of a gutter manufacturing company were asked this question by railway workers after a railway freight car was parked on a side track and nobody claimed to be the owner for several weeks.

Of course, the railway employees had looked inside. It was full of copper piping and sheets, and they found it strange that nobody was missing so much material. Because they presumed that there **must have been some administrative mistake**, they contacted the company that they thought could be the owner of the cargo.

They were surprised to learn that its management didn't know anything about it and they certainly weren't missing a train car full of copper. Their accounting didn't indicate that the container or cargo belonged to them, and none of their competent employees knew anything about it either. Only one thing was clear as day: it couldn't have been parked on the side track without someone putting it there.

Whose is the treasure?

As it couldn't stay there forever, a big investigation started. There weren't many factories in the region that used copper. The cargo was actually perfectly suited to the company manufacturing gutters.

So, its management decided to help the railway investigators and offered to buy the material if, once the owner was found, it proved to be uneconomical to send it to the original destination if the car had arrived there by mistake, for example.

But it all had an unexpected ending. When the company owner asked the dispatch manager to call some relevant companies to ask them about the ownership of the material in the car, the employee **started behaving very strangely**. He started trembling and faltering, which immediately attracted increased attention from the boss. Eventually, he didn't need to make any phone calls.

Stashed away material

The nervous dispatch manager confessed to everything. For three years, **he and the production manager** had been pilfering tiny untraceable parts of cargoes that could be written off as allowable deviations. Sometimes they even forged records of rejection rates increasing them artificially, even though it meant the production manager lost his bonuses. He knew that it would eventually pay off. And it did: little by little they "saved up" a freight container full of material.

All they needed then was to find a buyer on the black market via the Internet. As soon as they had found one and agreed on the price, they forged the relevant documentation and ordered a railway freight car to transport their copper treasure. But, as it was black market trade, **the buyer was hesitant to disclose his real name and address**. While he was trying to figure out where the goods could safely be delivered, the freight car was visible for so long that it aroused undesired attention at the departure station before it could get anywhere.

What is the lesson to be learnt?

- Whatever you call it – **embezzlement, document forgery or theft** – the aim of dishonest employees is to improve their situation at the expense of their employers.
- Sometimes a petty offence may gnaw so heavily at an employee's conscience that they never do it again. At other times, it may be the first step towards organized **crime of monumental proportions**.
- Nevertheless, it is always primarily up to you, the employer, to safeguard your property and business well and to **proactively** defend yourself from such deceivers.

Remember:

- When it comes to the inventiveness of some employees who are looking for money, there are really no boundaries.
- Especially if your company manufactures or trades something, you should focus closely on building surveillance and employee monitoring.
- Perform random checks and don't be afraid to implement unusual methods (I know of a company working with precious metals that even weighs its employees when they enter and leave the factory: if the difference is too big, a check is performed).
- Limit the number of employees who get in contact with material that can be stolen. This way you will limit the group of possible culprits.
- Let any dishonest employees clearly know that you are not going to tolerate any crimes or minor offences.
- Take a close look at your security staff as well: even they may be a source of theft!

IN CONCLUSION

The stories in this chapter, although quite different from each other, indicate that every single employee, regardless of age, position or years they have worked for your company, poses a potential risk, and you need to protect yourself from such risks.

Don't underestimate the importance of internal rules and control mechanisms that can help you reveal attempted or ongoing theft or embezzlement.

Chapter VII:

Two heads are better than one – teamwork

As you might have noticed in several previous stories, employees usually cause more damage to their employer if they find a partner in crime. Working as a team, they can think up a more sophisticated and highly-developed system of embezzlement, while covering each other's backs and erasing the evidence more effectively.

That makes it much more difficult for the employer to reveal such dirty business, and dismissing a large number of employees at once could paralyze the company's operations. Anyway, what such employers should realize is that if a team of people manages to circumvent or misuse the system, it is not the failure of an individual, but of the whole environment. And that's exactly where an error should be looked for in the first place: in the system.

Warehouse pals

If the employer in the following story hadn't had a **good monitoring system**, this gang of rogues would have probably caused much more damage. This story is a good example of how beneficial monitoring systems can be. These three young guys didn't reckon they could ever get caught, so they proceeded with absolute self-confidence.

I've already mentioned the necessity of having everything secured several times and I'm still far from finished. If need be, I can repeat it a thousand times: don't underestimate your security. **People are very inventive and some really know no boundaries**, just as the following story shows.

Place: **Czech Republic**

Main characters:

Victim: the owner of a food and drink warehouse	**Employee no. 1:** Jan, warehouse worker
	Employee no. 2: Pepa, warehouse worker
	Employee no. 3: Evžen,warehouse worker
	Customers

The magic of warehouses

Stores and warehouses are very unique places. Typically, there are a lot of pallets containing various goods. Warehouse workers transport these pallets from one place to another, preparing them for shipment or try to find the right place for new ones so that they aren't in the way. A warehouse is a bustling place and it is routine to see one warehouse worker transporting goods one way as his colleague transports goods the other.

Physical stocktaking normally requires that the warehouse be closed for some time, which is why stocktaking doesn't take place very often, since it means a loss of money. Furthermore, some pallets with boxes may get damaged, other goods are no longer sold, there are remainders of stock, some goods have passed their shelf lives and sometimes suppliers send the wrong stuff. Customers also make returns, which results in having various remainders, returned items and other goods in the warehouse that don't actually count towards the current stock. All these aspects complicate physical stocktaking.

One theft after another

Chaos is commonplace in many warehouses. As a place containing goods of great value, it is an environment that is almost begging to be misused. Even more so when the warehouse workers feel undervalued for their hard, manual labour, especially in terms of money. One complains to another about how hard life is; then they talk a little and come up with a plan.

Employers are lucky if it starts and ends with goods of little value that have expired or been discarded. Some things that get "lost" might be items that nobody was supposed to look for and aren't missed. Unfortunately, warehouse workers often go much further. Unless **they're deterred by security measures that a wise owner has put in place**, they can stop at nothing. I could tell you dozens of stories that are very similar to the one I'm going to tell you now. This type of fraud is really very common and it is up to employers to decide what use they are going to make of this information.

Let's fill some lorries

Warehouses storing food and drink contain thousands of items, and huge amounts of goods move in and out on a daily basis. One of the things that needs to be watched out for is the expiration date, so certain losses are quite normal. However, when stocktaking revealed that pallets of chewing gum and drinks that would have been enough to fill two lorries were missing, the owner found it rightfully suspicious.

Fortunately for him, he had the entire premises monitored by a camera surveillance system, so he watched the video recordings in search of the answer. Everything looked normal, there were no unauthorized people. The only activity he could see was warehouse workers stocking out goods as usual. However, the owner knew exactly which goods he should focus on. And what he saw was rather upsetting.

Everything has a buyer

Twenty-seven-year-old Jan, thirty-year-old Pepa and thirty-five-year-old Evžen worked on the same shift. The video recordings showed that they were the ones who most often dispatched the missing items. They were in no particular hurry or stressed out and proceeded as usual, so nobody suspected them of anything.

But in fact, **they were selling their employer's goods under his name illegally**. A pallet here, a pallet there, sometimes only small boxes. All the transactions looked absolutely legitimate, with the exception that the paperwork was just for effect because of the cameras. Once they left the warehouse the papers had to be destroyed.

Their fun lasted for about half a year, before the party was over and the thievish trio was revealed. The damage was more than 400,000 Czech crowns. The three warehouse workers ended up in court along with the **customers who had bought the goods from them for low prices, despite knowing they were stolen**. The customers were charged with the offence of "handling stolen goods". So the discount they got wasn't that great after all.

But that's not what matters most to us here. We're currently focusing on employees who are villains. I mentioned the punishment for the accomplices so that you realize that there must always be some other party involved: the case wasn't only about the employees-turned-thieves, it highlighted the fact that it was easy for them to sell the stolen goods.

If you hear someone saying “a lorry full of bubble gum was stolen”, it sounds absurd. However, even absurd things happen sometimes. That’s one more reason why you should **protect your – meaning your company’s – property with due care**, even if you think that your goods are unlikely to become the object of a crime. In this case, the employer was lucky to have a good camera surveillance system in place, thanks to which the crooks were eventually caught and convicted.

What is the lesson to be learnt?

- **Keeping records** of the goods you receive and dispatch should be the **alpha and omega** of your business. The best way to do this is to have an automated system that reads the bar code on each product and automatically adds or deducts it from the stock records.

- As this story has shown, it pays to invest in **a camera surveillance system**. If you have a number of cameras, you don’t need to watch the recordings one by one: it is a good idea to have them concentrated at one surveillance station where they are watched non-stop by trained staff or the recordings are archived and checked only when the situation requires. Nevertheless, you must make sure that the cameras are used **exclusively for watching your goods and property**! They shouldn’t be installed in places such as toilets or changing rooms, with respect to the protection of privacy. You should also inform your **employees** about the cameras with signs reading “This area is monitored by a camera system”.

- You might want to consider taking **some additional safety measures** – for instance, internal labelling of goods. What may be a significant deterrent is the employment of **security**

staff or some other supervisory force: individuals who are to be held liable for a great part of the damage, and such people will be aware of all the risks and consequences should anything get stolen. Sadly, small companies often think that paying security workers is a waste of money. That may be because **there are no records of the value of the goods that WEREN'T stolen**.

- There is **one thing that should be implemented universally**, not only in cases like the one described above. That is an **ethical code**. **I recommend that ALL employers** introduce one in their companies, define it clearly and insist that everyone adheres to it. It is important that your employees:

  1. know what the owner and company management's *attitude towards dishonest conduct* is,
  2. *adhere to the rules* and are aware that there is a zero-tolerance policy, and
  3. are informed about *the punishment and sanctions* they will b e subjected to if they do anything illegal.

- Research shows that it doesn't work if you believe that your employees will automatically adhere to the rules of decent conduct. It is necessary **to define boundaries and make sure they are followed**. The same research indicated that 40 per cent of employees breach work rules repeatedly.

Remember:

- **Make the most of technology that can keep track of the goods you have in stock and that cannot be fooled by an employee: bar code readers, radio frequency identification (RFID) chips and a camera surveillance system that archives recordings.**

- If you discover any dirty business, it is a good idea to impose exemplary punishments rather than sweeping it under the carpet, so that everyone sees you are uncompromising when it comes to such conduct.
- In some cases, the best option is to use specialized security services.
- Always have an ethical code in place and regularly remind your employees of its existence so that they know that no criminal activity will be tolerated.

A tonne or so of meat

We're going to continue with warehouses so that I can tell you about another rather common method of embezzlement that is so tempting in this environment. This story shows that sometimes things are different than they seem at first sight, and the person you initially suspect may actually be completely innocent.

Once again, it matters what safety measures and control mechanisms the company owner puts in place. Even in this case, where the truth came out eventually, the company's good reputation, under which both of the main characters acted, was severely damaged. Well, see for yourself.

Place: **Slovakia**

Main characters:

Victim no. 1: Laco, warehouse owner	×	**Employee no. 1:** Ján, driver, employee of the haulage company
Victim no. 2: haulage company owner		**Employee no. 2:** Štefan, the driver's assistant, employee of the haulage company

Outsourcing comes in handy

Laco supplied big food chains with meat and other food. As all the goods needed to be delivered early in the morning and then the fleet and drivers were idle, he calculated that it wasn't economical to buy cars. So he concluded a bilaterally advantageous contract with a haulier in the vicinity who regularly and reliably delivered his goods.

In reality, it meant that Ján, the driver, together with his assistant Štefan, showed up at the food warehouse every morning where the warehouse workers had all the goods prepared for them according to the orders and Ján and Štefan loaded them onto their lorry themselves. They didn't need anyone's help, they had professional equipment.

It went on like this for some time. Ján and Štefan knew the staff working in the warehouse well, so it was normal for them to take strolls around the premises, exchange a few words with friends, discuss family matters, plans and experiences, tell some jokes or arrange an evening out to play cards and drink beer.

A hapless victim

When Laco found out about a large deficit in warehouse stock, he logically gave the warehouse workers a hard time about it. They were the ones to be held liable for the warehouse, and they who had unrestricted access to the goods.

However, an investigation showed that the stock keepers were innocent. The culprits had actually come from the outside. Ján and Štefan **observed how insufficiently the warehouse was safeguarded for a long time before they came up with a plan that they were not shy to implement**.

In addition to the goods that they were supposed to dispatch according to orders and invoices, they repeatedly loaded – without anyone noticing – boxes of frozen meat, which they **immediately sold at lower prices** to restaurants or retailers. They delivered the stolen merchandise using their employer's official branded van for several months. They stole several tonnes of meat worth almost 10,000 euros.

Casting a shadow over their reputation

Both of the thieves ended up in court. **The thefts had affected two owners of two different companies**, although the culprits only worked for one of them. The warehouse owner paid dearly for his gullibility and lack of safety measures, which proved fatal.

The transport company's **reputation was damaged** and **it lost a long-standing customer**. As the word spread among other customers, its owners had a hard time making things right again, winning back customer confidence and saving the company from bankruptcy.

This summary contains the answer to the unvoiced question of what both entrepreneurs should have done differently in order to avoid such a situation.

What is the lesson to be learnt?

I appeal to you yet again to have:

- **sophisticated security measures in place and use information systems for dispatching and record keeping,**
- **monitoring systems, and**
- **even security staff if necessary.**

Nobody should have the chance to take anything away from your business without a written record being made and a responsible person knowing about it. Control mechanisms should concern not only buildings, but also vehicles used for business purposes. If you have a transport company, make sure that mileage is duly reported in the logbook and don't tolerate private activities.

Remember:

- Warehouse owners should take all precautions necessary in order to protect dispatched goods. It is very helpful to have a sophisticated information system and bar code or RFID chip readers.
- Owners of haulage companies should monitor the movement of their cars and employees using, for instance, GPS.
- If the two owners in this story had done these things, the goods wouldn't have been stolen and the haulage company's reputation wouldn't have been damaged.

A hard coal age

Now here's another group of employees who made a great team and robbed their employer. You've probably noticed that **groups usually cause much more damage than individuals**. It seems that the old saying "unity is strength" applies.

As for employees who unite against their employer, what they do has nothing to do with a romantic vision of resistance. Another complication is **that while an individual saboteur is easier to reveal, in an organized gang everyone covers each other's backs**.

Obviously, it is also easier to get even with an individual than with a larger number of people. You can read about what an organized pack of employees can devise in the following story.

Place: **Poland**

Main characters:

Victim: power company	**Employees:** an organized group of employees

A well-organized pack

The story I'm going to tell you took place in a large electricity company, which sold electric power and coal. One would think that it would be impossible to steal either of those and that suspecting employees of such a thing would be paranoid.

I can tell you at the very start that they succeeded in doing so. True, a whole bunch of well-tuned employees was needed. They were much better at illegal cooperation than the legal version. Some of the employees teamed up and sold coal on the side to other companies for more than a year. They sold the coal for lower prices than their employer was offering, so it seemed to be advantageous for all parties involved.

Thanks for the internal audit!

When the fraud was revealed and the investigation initiated, the inventiveness and genius exerted by the entire gang of employees came to light. That also explained why it took so long before clouds started gathering above their illegal activity and thwarted their future plans.

The strange thing was that the **embezzled goods were apparently sold with proper documentation**. However, a closer investigation discovered that many of the documents **didn't correspond with those approved and signed by the company's management**. Naturally, these documents included a large number of fake invoices.

As I've already written, everything seemed to be legitimate at first sight. And nobody had even reported suspected sales of stolen coal. Everything was revealed rather by chance: the case was initiated by **the internal auditor**. If it hadn't been for the audit, the damage could have been much worse. Still, the cost was exorbitant, exceeding five million dollars.

Since the crime took place rather recently, I have had to change the location of the story: at the time of writing, the details, results and conclusions of this case had not been publicized yet. Even with the little information I had at hand, I could still deduce certain conclusions that you can benefit from. My observations are included in the following text.

What is the lesson to be learnt?

- **Big companies** are **many times more likely** to become victims of fraudulent employees than **small companies** where there is not so much anonymity. Logically, this is linked to **the amount of possible losses**.

- **Internal audits** should be one of the most important control mechanisms; **external audits** should only follow afterwards. If you are not sure whether you can do it yourself and you suspect that you're losing money because of disloyal employees, you should invest in the **services of professional investigators** (forensic and investigation services) who have extensive experience with such situations.

- The best known of them, the **Association of Fraud Examiners (ACFE)**, has published numerous studies and releases conclusions and recommendations on what types of risks employers can anticipate and how to reveal and deal with them. I write in greater detail about this organization in the first chapter of the conclusion entitled "ACFE".

Remember:

▶ The bigger your company is, the harder you are going to have to fight the inventiveness of dishonest employees. It is likely that they won't act as solo-players but rather as a well-tuned team;

- the more often you will have to perform internal audits;
- and the more money you will need to invest in the protection of your property, but it certainly pays.

▶ **As I've mentioned previously, don't hesitate to have employees rotate jobs sometimes – and move them around to prevent stereotypes and repeated theft.**

Unparalleled cooperation of life gamblers

If an employer loses goods and property, like in the previous case, of course it is unpleasant, and it may prove to be a serious or even fatal problem for a company. However, there are business spheres where peculiar teamwork may result in much more serious damage: to clients' health and even lives.

Money aside, the real threat here is years spent in prison as well as lifelong scars on an entrepreneur's soul. The following story took place at a state-owned company, which probably multiplied the monstrous extent of the consequences, although the truth is that we often hear of similar cases of inhumanity from the private sector, too.

Place: **Portugal**

Main characters:

Victim no. 1: the state, the operator of a senior housing facility **Victim no. 2:** Juana, a client of a senior housing facility **Victims 3+:** other clients	×	**Employees:** a cunning team of carers including a doctor

Lack of strength and money

In the lives of many elderly people there comes a moment when it is no longer safe for them to live in their homes on their own, without supervision and care. Many of them don't have children who can take them into their homes and care for them, or they feel that they would be a bother to them.

They come to the logical conclusion that the best solution is to start using the services of some specialized social care facilities. There are retirement homes that provide care to those who are self-sufficient and just need someone to keep an eye on them and assist when required. There are also facilities that offer constant health care, catering, laundry, personal hygiene assistance and other services, depending on the individual's condition and abilities.

While confined to her hospital bed, recovering from a hip fracture, Juana, a childless elderly lady, decided that a care home would be the best place to move to when she was discharged. She hadn't saved much money for retirement, so private nursing homes were out of question. She had lived a rather modest life and wasn't used to luxury, so she didn't feel worried when nurses arranged for her to be transported to a state-owned facility whose services were at the cheaper end of what was available.

The only thing she was afraid of was solitude. The home was rather far from where she had lived before and where she had at least a few friends who could come to see her every now and then. Most of them were of an advanced age like her, so she couldn't expect them to travel far to see her.

The early warning signs

Juana knew that it wouldn't be easy to get used to the new environment. When the ambulance took her to a rather dismal old building, the time spent waiting at reception seemed endless.

From her mobile bed all she could do was watch the gloomy doorway and listen to stony silence, only occasionally interrupted by the sound of a bell ringing in the nurse's room or a muffled groan. She knew that pain was, sadly, inseparable from this stage of life, but she still couldn't get rid of the icy feeling that these sounds would become a permanent part of the rest of her life.

When a nurse eventually opened the reception and went through the transport documentation with the medic, she seemed to be reserved and didn't say a single word to Juana. She did everything she had to and showed the attendant where to take the new client. A couple of minutes later Juana was in her new bed and watched the door close behind him. Dead silence fell again.

Endless waiting

She had made a long journey to get there and had waited a long time in the reception area of her new home, so Juana, who had drunk half a pot of tea for breakfast, realized that she would soon need assistance. She wasn't used to the embarrassing feeling of asking for help when she needed to go to the toilet.

But the last couple of weeks spent in the hospital had taught her that she had no other option, so she looked for a bell to call a nurse. Unfortunately, the cord with the button was on the other side of the night table, out of her reach, so she hoped that someone would come soon to welcome her and explain how things worked there and at that point she would ask for a bedpan.

More than an hour passed. The urge to use the toilet started causing Juana pain and nobody had showed up. She had no other choice but to call for help. She hopelessly raised her voice and after a while she broke into tears, overwhelmed by all the emotions. At that moment the door burst open and there was the same unfriendly nurse who had received her. She looked very angry.

"Well, that's a start, madam! You cannot go on like this, shouting all over the place, you're not alone here!" she shouted at Juana. In answer to her request for a bedpan she replied: "I'll tell the colleague who's coming in half an hour. My shift is almost over and I still have some paperwork to fill in and you're disturbing me. You can wait for a while, you're not a small child."

Helplessly waiting for death

When Juana's neighbour Marisa came to see her after two months wanting to check whether the nursing home would be the right choice for her one day, she couldn't believe her eyes. The employee who turned up in the doorway looked very surprised when she asked him for Juana's room number.

Instead of her friend she found a poor human wreck, skinny and totally dehydrated. Juana was lying in her own excrements and staring apathetically at the ceiling. When she saw Marisa, a tear rolled down her cheek.

Marisa started pressing the bell desperately, calling for help. But there was no response to the incessant buzzing. She ran to the nurse's office, shouting to them to call the doctor. She met that same man again who told her that the doctor wasn't there at the moment but if there was a problem he could try to call him.

A shocking revelation

Marisa didn't wait, she called an ambulance. The man in the doorway tried to stop her promising that he could see to that, but Marisa ignored him. She described over the phone what a bad condition Juana was in, and the ambulance operators contacted the police and asked them to attend with them.

Then things moved rather quickly. Even the seasoned policemen were astonished by the condition in which they found the clients, so they contacted social welfare and the deputy of the regional operator of the home.

An inspection revealed that the employees had set their own rules. There should have been six of them plus a doctor on each shift, but since they were dissatisfied with their low salaries for such hard work, they had found a way to make an extra buck. However, their collaboration had evolved into something unbelievable.

Every day there was **only one employee who came to clock in and fill in the relevant documents for all the staff**.

Meanwhile, the others worked elsewhere and didn't care in the slightest that they were being paid to do their regular job the entire time.

The employee who got the short end of the stick that day could hardly check all the clients and handed out food on the fly. By the time the last meals were served, they were usually cold. After some time, the attendant took the trays away and didn't care if the meals remained untouched because the patients needed assistance or couldn't reach them. There was not enough time to hold a straw to help them drink either, let alone regular hygiene and other assistance.

The only nurse at work spent most of the time **filling in daily records with fabricated items of care for the seniors** and matching them with the names of those who were supposed to have worked during the shift that day. At the end of the shift one employee clocked out for everyone and another one picked up the baton. **That meant that the clients only got medical attention when it was a doctor's turn to take the shift**. But even the doctors were busy with other things anyway and couldn't fully attend to the patients' needs.

Night shifts were much calmer for the unscrupulous employees because they didn't have to go to the trouble of serving food. They slept in the nurse's office in case the phone rang or some of the clients called for assistance.

But later on, the patients even gave up on that as they didn't dare to disturb the unfriendly staff. As most of the seniors either didn't have children who would come to see them or their children lived far away and were okay with just hearing reassuring news about them from time to time, they were literally waiting to die in isolation, and they actually wished death would be merciful and come as soon as possible.

The finale

Thanks to Marisa's visit, Juana was soon in the care of doctors at a nearby hospital. Unfortunately, her body was far too weak, and despite all the medical care she received, her kidneys failed in a couple of days and the inevitable followed.

It is hard to say how much the neglect in the nursing home contributed to her sudden departure: there was nobody to sue the home and insist that everything be investigated. If there's no plaintiff, there's no case.

The administrator made things right immediately by sacking all the employees and hiring new ones while appointing obligatory non-stop supervision, but a thorough investigation of Juana's case would have only attracted more media attention, which would have been detrimental to an institution that was trying to get back on its feet.

What is the lesson to be learnt?

- Here I can return to the **theory of the Fraud Triangle** described in the Introduction. As you know, it consists of **motivation, opportunity and rationale**. You can easily find all three of these components in this case.

- And I will reemphasize what has been written a million times: **don't underestimate the need for supervision**. Don't imagine that your employees will consider your or your clients' interests more important than theirs, that you can blindly rely on any of them or that all people working in social services must automatically be selfless angels who feel an incessant urge to help others.

- Especially in industries where human health or even lives are at stake, you should be **doubly cautious and watch out for any failures on the part of your employees** as the consequences may be fatal. The early warning signs in this case could have been any discomfort perceived by the seniors; much more serious signs would include health issues or even death caused by negligence.

- Supervise and monitor, make use of the high-tech devices available and, last but not least, choose your employees carefully, motivate them, train them and **reward them for working well while not overlooking their bad work**. It is easier said than done, I know. But business is sometimes a hard game to play.

Remember:

- The more freedom employees have the more prone they are to adjust the rules to their liking. And sometimes they even fail to adhere to the basic ones.

- The same can be said of remote workplaces where employees are not supervised. Therefore, you should visit such places regularly and once in a while you should do a "raid" when nobody expects you to show up so you get to see what customers would see.

- Get your employees involved in increasing not only economic results, but in the case of services also customer satisfaction. A part of their salaries should be variable, based on the percentage of satisfaction achieved.

- **Don't focus only on hard data, such as attendance, but check in person how your staff approach customers and clients. Perform random checks and use mystery shoppers to get a better picture of the actual status quo.**
- **Don't just settle for a description of the current situation on the phone, seeing is believing.**

IN CONCLUSION

Although the last story will probably send shivers down your spine if you think about it too long, believe me that such things happen and, unfortunately, quite often.

Some dishonest employees proceed with incredible ease and insolence, especially when they are not alone. Two heads are better than one, they say – so the theft or fraud can be thought out more thoroughly.

When they don't have to hide what they are doing because they are covering each other's backs, they are much calmer and more inconspicuous, which plays into their hands, too. So, you shouldn't lose vigilance just because there's a friendly atmosphere at work.

Chapter VIII:

You scratch my back and I'll scratch yours – bribery and corruption

Offenders can often do without a co-conspirator in the family, but they generally need an accomplice from the outside. Somebody who will avert their eyes, protect them, make false documents or otherwise help the thieves accomplish their goals.

What is the best way to motivate somebody to become an accomplice? Such people need to be interested, so they are influenced by bribery or another form of corruption that provides an advantageous counter-service.

Driving licence while you wait

We discussed forging documents when I described the cases of those who were more or less professional forgers. But business can be done even with genuine documents, as is evidenced by the occasional cases that appear in the media when such a fraud is revealed. For instance, those who have graduated from ten-minute study programmes could tell tales about that.

The following story shows that we can come across such maladies even in the private sector. This time it is not about employees forging documents for themselves. It is about a man who forges documents for others who offer to pay for his "work" – an example of supply meeting demand to the detriment of the company owner.

Place: **Slovakia**

Main characters:

Victim: Denis, owner of a driving school	**Employee:** Julius, driving school instructor

In the hands of a pro

Every driver knows that first you need to spend many hours listening to theory, then do the driving lessons and then do a lot of studying for the tests. Then D-day comes, when you demonstrate whether you have what it takes to join the other drivers on the road. It is not unusual for somebody to fail the tests and then have to retake them.

Julius was happy to become an instructor and liked his job at first. He used to be a professional driver and had actually never done much other than turn the steering wheel. However, after some time, he started to become fed up with teaching his new students the same stuff over and over again.

Moreover, some students were incorrigible. They repeatedly made the same simple mistakes, they were not able to use the clutch correctly, the engine cut out every time they started the car at a crossroads and they behaved like they knew it all, even better than their instructor. No matter how hard he tried to teach them the driving regulations, they always made so many mistakes on the tests that he felt like biting their heads off. Well, being an instructor at a driving school was not all fun and games.

But he didn't know what else he could do. He was well aware that the job for the driving school was a secure and cushy number. Nobody cared much about where he drove during the day, so he could run many of his own errands while getting paid for it. And people will always need driving licences.

Increase in demand

When the demand for driving licences suddenly increased rather significantly, Denis, the owner of the driving school, began to rack his brains as to what could have caused the change. As far as he knew, there was no government amendment in the pipeline that would complicate passing the exams in the future.

Nevertheless, it was good news for his business, so he stopped caring about the reason and looked forward to higher profits instead. He usually sent potential clients directly to Julius who would make all the necessary arrangements with them. Profits were on the rise, although not dramatically, so Denis rubbed his hands together in delight.

A bad joke

After a couple of months, people around him started making double-edged allusions that he didn't understand. He ignored them at first, but more and more people poked at him until one day a friend of his asked him directly how much he would have to pay to get a driving licence for his daughter without her having to learn anything or wait.

Denis considered it a very bad joke. However, his friend looked serious and after Denis refused to engage in such nonsense, he kept bidding up his price and wouldn't take no for an answer. The friend cut off the conversation by angrily asking how it was that Denis could do it for strangers but not for him.

Churning out the licences

After this, Denis looked more carefully Julius and it soon all dawned on him. Julius claimed that at the start there was a rich student who had slipped a quite modest amount of money in his pocket so that he would excuse her from the rest of the obligatory driving that she found useless as she could drive already. Then she asked him with a smile whether he could help her a little with the tests. One word led to another and they agreed on a deal.

This all resulted in Julius having an unofficial price list so that he didn't have to bargain with everyone individually time after time. Talking to people annoyed him to death, so all he needed to do was to show them the price list and they chose the items they wanted to buy. He had a rate for excusing an hour of driving, a rate for successfully passing the tests and so on. Later, he needed to expand his portfolio of services, so he hired for his "business" a good friend who was a policeman, and they split the remuneration for successfully passing the practical part of the test.

So, this driving school was selling driving licences one after another without the students doing anything. When there was a new inquiry, Julius first checked the client to find out what he could dare to offer. He took on some of them officially, so as not to awaken suspicion, and only sold them "relief" from the endless hours spent on driving lessons. Other candidates were presented with his special offer.

The clients who paid him for their driving licences never complained. They were happy they could pass the exam effortlessly and without wasting time. There was mutual satisfaction.

What Julius forgot to take into consideration was that word of his practices could spread. People share lots of information without thinking about how far it may get. Ordinary gossip was the weakest link in the chain that proved fatal for his "business" and put an end to it. As one would expect, there was also an aftermath for the policeman involved.

Because of this unpleasant revelation, Denis lost his trust in people, his reputation and almost even his legitimate business.

What is the lesson to be learnt?

- This is a typical example of how corruption works on any scale. If we want to illustrate what **bribery** is, we don't necessarily have to point to politics.
- Strictly speaking, even if Julius had received **boxes of chocolate instead of money** it would still count as bribery under the law.
- His actions damaged the good reputation of his employer and his company.
- Furthermore, those who issue unearned diplomas, certificates or any other official documents may be prosecuted, which can result in them being banned from doing business and so on.

Remember:

- Regularly assess whether your company gives your employees opportunity for corruption.
- Corruption in your company will easily damage its good name and position on the market and can even result in bankruptcy.
- It is also advisable to introduce a way for anyone to notify you of unfair practices in your company by establishing anonymous "suggestion boxes".

Game over

There are other ways your employees may arrange special agreements involving bribery behind your back. There are many other lethal combinations, for instance dishonest employees.

Read for yourself what happens in the following story about what a single saboteur in conspiracy with another person can do, and how many people can be deceived before the least suspicion arises.

Place: **USA**

Main characters:

Victim: Chris, company owner	×	**Employee:** James, manager of the customer complaints department **Client:** a customer with a surprisingly great deal of bad luck

A fountain of complaints

James, who worked as the head of customer complaints for Chris's company, was swamped with work. One of their biggest and most significant customers suddenly had more and more reasons to file complaints, which was very unpleasant for both parties involved. Naturally, the company didn't want to lose such a big customer, but the management found it very suspicious that the flaws occurred almost exclusively with this client and so frequently.

Chris repeatedly sent James out to the customer to **thoroughly investigate whether the complaints were legitimate**. He didn't want to rely on junior staff. James was the most experienced employee Chris had for this job, and he was capable of coping with issues and faults on site. Unfortunately, all the complaints proved to be justified and the flaws were irremediable, which meant that all the complaints filed by this customer had to be acknowledged. The customer was probably just unlucky as all the faulty products were shipped to him by mere coincidence, Chris thought.

Consequently, Chris had to pay contractual sanctions over and over again and his best customer was becoming, slowly but surely, the least profitable one. After some months the business with that customer even resulted in financial loss. This was odd, as the cooperation had worked just fine before.

It didn't occur to anyone to suspect James of having something to do with it. It was in his interest to protect his employer's good name. Moreover, the bonuses for the customer complaints department were conditioned by keeping the number of accepted complaints as low as possible. He couldn't influence the quality of the goods delivered, but if the flaws could have been fixed during his inspection or defined so that they could be prevented next time, he would certainly have made sure of it. But his thorough checks always revealed new, justified and irremediable defects.

Trust but check

When the situation with this one customer didn't improve and the sanctions grew almost geometrically, Chris finally became suspicious. After ruling out a failure of the employees in manufacturing and of control mechanisms, he focused on the customer complaints department. Chris was reluctant to doubt James's competence to assess the situation correctly. After all, he was a long-standing and experienced employee.

But there must be something wrong! So Chris, his mind plagued by worries and questions, **went along with James to check another complaint**. However, that time – surprise, surprise – everything was alright. The customer failed to present the presumably faulty product and it was obvious that nobody had actually expected him to do so. After some amount of stammering, when neither the customer nor James was able to explain the situation, Chris wanted to see the products from the previously acknowledged complaints. As you have probably suspected, he wasn't presented with anything, so on their way back he put the squeeze on James.

James confessed to everything and Chris certainly wasn't happy to hear that James had a secret agreement with the customer about remuneration for each acknowledged complaint. **The bribes were larger than the bonuses he would have received from his employer**, and he didn't care about the fact that his colleagues lost their bonuses because of him.

Chris immediately parted ways with James as well as with the customer. James tried to get a job at his associate's company, but he was told that they weren't interested in such a dishonest employee.

What is the lesson to be learnt?

- When employees have certain key decision-making authority, there is always space for corruption and a risk that the authority will be misused. There is always a great degree of likelihood that such employees will go astray, either of their own will or by succumbing to a tempting offer presented by a third party.

- Personal benefits or interests **don't always have to be monetary**. Sometimes it is a **reciprocal service**, oftentimes it is a **promise** of things to come. One thing is for sure: if your employees take to this "pastime", there won't be any room for your interests.

Remember:

- ZIntroduce the four-eyes principle in your company, meaning that at least two people from different departments always have to agree on certain matters. This way you can effectively prevent fraudulent conduct and mutual agreements that aren't in your favour.

- ZPerform regular checks to uncover any situations that are not in line with your internal rules and processes.

- ZTake an interest in how well your employees represent your company. Participate in some negotiations yourself so that you know what actually happens there.

Sabotage from the inside

A whole book could be written solely about **tenders**. However, in this book we're going to focus on just one dimension of tenders: the damage that can be caused by dishonest employees.

Those who have some experience with tenders, and especially those for whom tenders are the daily bread and butter on which the future of their business depends, know how important trust and confidentiality are in this process. However, trust and confidentiality can be breached. And if it takes you too long to discover that, as in Václav's case, you can find yourself in big trouble.

Place: **Czech Republic**

Main characters:

Victim: Václav, owner and boss of an IT company	×	**Employee:** Evžen, an obliging IT guy

Rivalry, but not in all circumstances

It is commonplace in many industries that people from competing companies sometimes cooperate on certain projects. They don't necessarily want to cut each other's throats, they may even help each other, although all of them, quite logically, care primarily about their own interests. To be more precise, they care about their company's profit.

Václav and his employees knew this from their own experience. In the IT industry it is often necessary to split one order between companies because of the volume of work or the need to exchange specialists. After many years of useful collaboration, employees working for different companies often have very good relationships.

But one thing troubled Václav more and more. No matter how hard he tried, he couldn't win any interesting big tenders that would really help out his company. He always lost by just a little and he had to settle for one of his friendly competitors offering him at least partial cooperation on the project. However, the result of this was that he couldn't charge as much as if he had won such a tender himself.

An anonymous accusation

Just as Václav was going through the background documents of another unsuccessful tender, searching for an answer as to why he failed, he received a very interesting email. An anonymous writer informed him, apparently with good intentions, that Václav was nourishing a viper in his bosom, as he had a saboteur in his team who was far too close to his competition.

The search for that person didn't take long. Evžen was the only one who had above-par relationships with the companies that regularly won tenders. He had worked for Václav's company for more than six years and knew the ropes of the business. He was a real expert in his field and was happy to advise his colleagues whenever needed.

What Václav didn't know was that Evžen was so nice that he even helped **his colleagues when they were preparing final offers for tenders**. And he had no idea that this was not due to Evžen's good will or selflessness.

A job on the side

How can we define, with certain exaggeration, what Evžen did with the information he received? A part-time job? A source of extra income? Sabotage of his employer and his company? Make your choice.

It has probably occurred to you what Evžen's motivation really was. **He sold strictly confidential information** about what Václav's company was going to offer in tenders to competitors. The competition then **adjusted their final offers** according to this information so that they would win the tender – their offers were always slightly more advantageous, slightly cheaper.

Evžen had been helping out in this "unselfish" way **for three years** without arousing the slightest suspicion. The anonymous email arrived when he was about to start working for a competitor. But after he was exposed, the notice period was quickly reduced to the shortest time necessary for him to pack his things so that he couldn't harm the company any longer. And his employer-to-be also had second thoughts about hiring him.

To Evžen's dismay, the connections and friendly relationships between the two companies also existed at the management level, so Evžen's bad reputation preceded him before he could even start the new job.

What is the lesson to be learnt?

- The leakage of confidential information is still considered something theoretical or abstract, even though the damage caused by employees is, unfortunately, not negligible or rare. The truth is that entrepreneurs usually expect attacks to come from the outside, and **they tend to neglect internal protection of sensitive data**.

- The damage a company incurs may take many different forms. In the best-case scenario, it is only financial damage. In more serious cases **the long-term leakage of information may result in damage of a company's good reputation** or even **bankruptcy**.

- For the sake of objectivity, I should note that such leakage is not always due to over-talkative and disloyal employees or purposeful conduct, as was the case in this story. Often it is due to a lost flash drive or laptop, a weakly protected password, an email sent to the wrong address or printed materials that happened to catch someone's eye. There are almost limitless ways **in which data can leak out unintentionally**.

- **Data protection** should be of primordial importance. You should be protected not only against attacks from external hackers, but especially against those from within. You should restrict access to sensitive information and only grant it to employees with due authorization

- Data transfer in today's digitalized world is very fast and simple. You should realize that **transferring the entire database of your key customers takes seconds**, and the loss of such data is often catastrophic.

Remember:

▶ Regularly check the Internet browsers on all company devices. Keep tabs on what data your employees transfer and where. The best option is to prohibit them from accessing their private email accounts and to seal any USB ports so that they cannot leak data on flash drives.

- Only grant access to pivotal systems and databases to vetted and duly trained employees. Still, even they should be randomly checked.
- Always choose strong passwords for your systems, by which I mean you should use combinations of lower- and upper-case letters, numbers and special characters when possible. Passwords such as names of favourite films, children's names or dates of birth are always very risky as they are very easy to decipher. Also make sure that your employees don't have their passwords on their desks, notice boards or Post-it® notes stuck to their screens. Even that happens sometimes!
- Physical access to your archive of, for example, supply contracts or to sales department should also be granted to authorized personnel only.

Merry Christmas!

Do you give your customers, business partners, colleagues and employees Christmas presents as a thank you for their cooperation? And are you sure that they actually receive them?

Unless you **hand them the presents in person**, it is rather likely that a certain percentage of them ends up in someone else's hands, pockets or households.

Place: **Poland**

Main characters:

Victim: Lech, company owner	**Employee:** Andrzej, head of the marketing department

A different kind of Christmas shopping

Marketers know it well. Every year they need to go through catalogues of promotional items that look exactly the same as always and search for something new, original and of value for a reasonable price – something that will make clients, employees and business partners really happy. If you have ever tried to do this, you know what a thankless task it is.

So, Andrzej was honestly delighted when Lech, the company owner, announced that they would do something totally different that Christmas. They decided not to give their employees gifts with company logos on them as they had done before. They prepared a surprise for them, which they were positive would not end up in the bin or be regifted to someone else.

Lech decided that the present would be **gift-vouchers for buying goods at the supermarket worth 300 zlotys** (around 70 euros). Two hundred vouchers, to be precise. In addition to the vouchers, Andrzej had a storeroom full of other gifts such as bottles of wine, T-shirts, sleeping bags and belts with the company logo on them as well as more expensive items for more important clients and partners. That meant that he could fully focus on organizing their Christmas party.

Let it steal, let it steal, let it steal!

It was supposed to be a beautiful Christmas for everyone – merry and joyful. But when Lech asked several of his employees, shortly after returning to work in the new year, how happy they were with the Christmas presents from him, he noticed their ironic grimaces as they politely thanked him while exchanging questioning looks.

So, Lech asked more questions and found out that his employees had received quite different presents from those he had intended for them. When a few of them showed him the funny multi-coloured pens that were left over from a summer marketing event for customers, he immediately called the head of marketing.

Andrzej was smart enough, so he presented his boss with several receipts for refreshments and **told him a story about several banquets** for employees who preferred having a Christmas party to receiving a gift-voucher. He might have got away with it if this information hadn't got to the ears of the employees and Andrzej's colleagues, the ones who were supposed to have had so much fun at the parties.

Christmas gifts for everyone

It came to light that the only party that actually took place was a festive Christmas party for Andrzej's family and friends. Andrzej actually spent the gift-vouchers in his own special way.

He only used a few of them do his own shopping. But as he was no gullible risk-taker and he wanted to cover his back in case the boss asked, he shopped in a clever way. Boxes and packages of alcohol and soft drinks, lots of coffee, hampers – everything that qualified as "refreshments" – and the relevant receipts could be used as evidence of the Christmas parties.

Most of the vouchers ended up in hands they were not meant for. When shopping, Andrzej led the shop assistants to believe that he got too many of them at work and couldn't spend them all, so he offered them lucrative deals. **He was willing to sell them vouchers worth 300 zlotys for only 200.**

Many shop assistants nodded happily to such an offer, as they had big Christmas shopping lists ahead and they liked the idea of getting a third off all their purchases. Andrzej usually talked them into buying more vouchers for their colleagues, family and friends, so he only had to go to six nearby supermarkets before the vouchers were gone and his pocket was stuffed with banknotes. He could finally go and buy luxury presents – not for his colleagues, but for his family.

The final bell tolls

I suppose you won't be surprised to hear that Andrzej no longer works for that company. He should consider himself lucky that Lech decided that he would be **okay with damage compensation** and didn't take him to court. So, Andrzej paid the full value of the vouchers. He could have pulled his hair out – instead of having his Christmas spree paid for by the company, he actually subsidized the Christmas joy of some shop assistants.

What is the lesson to be learnt?

- Embezzlement doesn't always have to be about stealing millions and it doesn't even have to bring your company down. Nevertheless, even **these small-time embezzlers should be caught as soon as possible**. The main character of this story actually supplied himself using company resources all the time when working as the head of marketing.

- Try to make a quick calculation of how big a loss he would have caused over ten years' time, even if the goods stolen each month were worth only 300 euros or so. Trust me, even small numbers **can add up to a decent sum**.

- That's why I advise you **not to underestimate the importance of record keeping**. Yes, **even of trivial items**. Be fair to your property and keep track of where it is, what is happening to it, when, under what circumstances and why it is leaving your company, and insist that everything is duly and verifiably logged.

Remember:

- Sometimes just a little effort is enough to put an end to a small-time thief's extra earnings: all you need to do is to communicate openly. In this story, it would have been sufficient if the company owner had sent all his employees an email thanking them for their effort that year and telling them that instead of an "umbrella" they would get a voucher that would certainly prove more useful.

- Don't give tricky employees any chance to misuse a situation. Check their work and ask them for all the relevant documents proving that they bought what they were supposed to and that the goods ended up where you intended.

- In some cases, it may even be better to leave it to a company that specializes in offering such services.

IN CONCLUSION

Humans are bribeable creatures by nature – and refusing to participate in corrupt conduct requires strong moral character. A necessary precondition for success is that the person feels fully appreciated, especially in terms of money.

If people don't feel like they need money, they can resist a tempting offer more easily and relish the gratifying feeling of having a strong will and good morals. They may even notify the authorities of such conduct.

As they say, everyone has their price. Generally speaking, employees come up with the idea of bribes as a form of extra earnings, but I've come across cases where employees damaged their employers because they became the victims of threats or blackmail. Hence you should be open to your employees and regularly check all the activities that occur in your company.

Chapter IX:

David and Goliath – abuse of power

Not every collaboration that includes fraudulent activity is necessarily deliberate on the part of everyone involved, or even beneficial. Some parties may not even be aware of the collaboration.

I am alluding to situations where employees misuse their position or power to their own benefit. Fraudsters have a heyday in this sphere too, so we shouldn't overlook such cases. They may cause big trouble to you, their employers.

Converting Cs to As

The best environment for the abuse of power is one where the victim is inferior to an obvious authority. Typically, fear takes over if the authority is also an "official".

What can help victims in such situations are street smarts and a sufficient amount of self-confidence. Sadly, the main character in the following story didn't have either of those. She was a young and very shy student who, instead of being able to focus on her studies, had to deal with another unexpected problem.

Place: **USA**

Main characters:

Victim no. 1:
a university

Victim no. 2:
Jessica,
student

Employee:
Richard,
mathematics
professor

A dream come true

When Jessica received a letter from her dream university informing her that she'd been accepted, she was on cloud nine and promised herself that she would be a diligent student – nothing in the world could prevent her from graduating. She didn't want to disappoint her parents who had struggled to get the money to pay for her studies. They considered their daughter's education of primary importance, and they were ready to tighten their belts so that she could afford it.

Jessica had been a willing and conscientious student in high school. The only thing she had had problems with was mathematics, despite all the extra lessons she took. She was also afraid of mathematics at university, so she made a resolution that she would do everything in her power to achieve the best results. As soon as she arrived at the university, she signed up for private tutoring from Richard, her professor. She had to work in a supermarket for several hours a week to afford it, but she was determined not to put her dream in jeopardy. Nothing in life is free.

A strange feeling

She soon discovered the truth in that statement. Her tutor was friendly right from the start, and it seemed that he cared about Jessica's marks just as much as she did. He went over everything with her in great detail and patiently explained to her how to use various formulas.

He spoke slowly in a calm voice, which soon started to make Jessica nervous. She didn't know why, but at times she had shivers down her spine and had an inexplicable bad feeling. After a couple of lessons, she realized she was afraid of Richard. In her mind, she started coming up with excuses why she couldn't go to the extra lesson and started to think it would be best to completely cancel the tutoring.

She was angry at herself. Her parents and even her professor didn't deserve to be let down like that for no reason. So, she gritted her teeth and convinced herself she had to go on attending the tutoring.

A high price

During one particular lesson, Richard tried to use an illustration to explain what a circumscribed circle is and he used their bodies as an example. He made her stand in front of him face to face, holding his hands, and he showed her circles while explaining to her in his forceful deep voice how it all worked.

Jessica felt very uncomfortable. She didn't have much experience with men and the physical proximity of her professor frightened her. She tried to break free, but he clenched her tighter and whispered in her ear that **if she were a good girl she wouldn't have to be afraid of mathematics at all**.

In no time his hands were under the distraught girl's blouse and tears were running down her cheeks. The professor was an authority and he was obviously stronger, so after crying all night long, she couldn't think of a better way out than quitting the extra lessons.

A devil's vengeance

Experienced Richard didn't leave anything to chance. After a lecture he asked her, in front of all the students, to help him take the teaching aids to his office. Poor Jessica couldn't refuse as she had no acceptable excuse for doing so.

She resignedly followed her professor and it happened again. Richard pounced on her, harassed her again **and threatened to give her bad marks if she didn't submit to his wishes**. He promised that if she docilely accommodated his lecherous proposals, she wouldn't have to study mathematics at all, she would be guaranteed the best marks for all the years to come.

Jessica cried and refused the offer, saying she would tell the university management everything. Richard pushed her away in disgust and growled that it would be his word against hers and nobody would believe her. After that, he didn't look even the slightest bit friendly.

Jessica was so scared that after moping around for a couple of weeks she suffered a nervous breakdown and had to be hospitalized. Thanks to expert care, she eventually spoke out about everything and the matter reached the dean.

A perverted system of marking

The investigation involved a university psychologist who over the next couple of days talked to all the female students who had private lessons with that professor. It came out that Jessica by far wasn't the first or only victim of Richard's harassment.

He selected only good-looking girls with large bosoms and offered them good marks in exchange for their sexual services. Some of them didn't hesitate. They were more experienced, and Richard was charming and rather handsome, so the prospect of saving a lot of time on studying boring mathematics was very tempting for them.

These days, this amorous professor probably gives remedial lessons to his fellow prisoners, although they don't have much to offer him in exchange. So we can hope that, at least now, he teaches mathematics by the rules.

What is the lesson to be learnt?

- **The abuse of power is as old as mankind**. There is no reason to believe that your employees will be the exception.

- **An authority or an official** from whom an applicant needs something may be even more tempted to misuse their position. **It is the fear** of people in superior positions that allows such people to misuse their powers.

- **The victims** of such abuse **often don't report it** because they feel ashamed, which means that the offenders can **continue to abuse their authority for a long time**. Moreover, the more one has, the more one wants, so they often raise their requirements.

Remember:

- Selecting employees is absolutely crucial since they are the face of your company. Their clothes matter as well as their communication style and behaviour. As I've mentioned several times before, you shouldn't underestimate references: find out as much information as you can about your future employees – for instance, why they quit their previous jobs.

- It is a good idea to conduct a survey of how satisfied your customers are with your employees from time to time. That way you can find out about situations similar to the one described above. It certainly pays to do it anonymously. But you definitely need to interpret the results in a wider context and ask other colleagues for their opinions, as such questionnaires may sometimes go adrift and provoke the assessor's revenge.

▶ You should also introduce a suggestion box that will help you reveal inappropriate behaviour at work, such as bullying, as soon as it starts.

Chinese Whispers

When two managers from two companies meet, it is not always to have a friendly chat over a cup of coffee. In the following story you're going to read about two managers who told each other much more than they were supposed to and, what is worse, much more than they were allowed to.

Place: **Austria**

Main characters:

Victim no. 1: a company traded on the stock exchange	**Employee no. 1:** Franz, a talkative manager
Victim no. 2: a company traded on the stock exchange	**Employee no. 2:** Johann, a talkative manager

A pair like no other

Two men are facing many years in prison for telling each other what should have remained the secrets of the companies they worked for. They were both top managers, and so they had access to a lot of interesting information.

Because they **exchanged top secret information**, Franz and Johann have now been charged with illegally making more than a million euros. They were found guilty of insider trading.

Shared secrets

The fact that the two gentlemen had access to sensitive information was nothing unusual, given the nature of their jobs. Franz and Johann were friends and they had a lot of opportunities to meet up, make a plan and implement it without anyone disturbing them.

Johann, representing a company whose stocks were publicly traded and that was going through times of instability, was the initiator. Because of the impending crisis, his company's results were volatile, which led Johann to an interesting thought. Franz immediately liked the idea too, and together they turned it into a detailed plan. As everyone knows, two heads are better than one: in business and even more so when cheating.

The two of them were on the same wavelength and they were emboldened **by the feeling that they were very important and untouchable**. Believing that they would not be subjected to any sanctions, they met for two months like secret agents to exchange confidential information.

This information concerned **quarterly performance reports and tenders won by their companies, which was reflected in the price of their stocks**. Simply put, depending on how each of the companies fared, its price on the stock exchange either rose or fell. Information of this kind can be smartly taken advantage of and cashed in on through buying and selling stocks.

Franz and Johann used a third party for their transactions: a company that bought their employers' stocks for them so that the buyer or seller was always a person who had nothing to do with the company. Then they split the money they earned in half and it went to their private accounts.

Similar situations, where **employees of big companies exchange sensitive information**, can occur at any time and in any industry.

What is the lesson to be learnt?

- Trading the stocks of a company that an employee has detailed information about, because of their job as a manager there, is a rather common problem.
- The misuse of information may take many different forms.
- For instance, an employee sets up a company by proxy of a relative while getting information from the employer about customers, suppliers and planned innovations of their products.
- Or, when terminating an employment contract, an employee takes, along with their final pay cheque, a whole range of information and sells it to the competition.

Remember:

- ▶ Protect all your company's sensitive data.
- ▶ Restrict the number of employees who have access to such information.

- Sign declarations of disinterestedness and confidentiality agreements with key employees, while stipulating sanctions for breaching them. A lot of information exchange takes place in response to the motto "what isn't prohibited is allowed", and if you clearly show your employees what punishment they'll be subject to, they will think twice before taking such a risk.

- If possible, include in your employment agreements, particularly those with managers, non-competitive clauses so that your employees cannot establish a competing company profiting from the information they acquired from you as soon as they leave.

- Introduce three levels of classified documents inside your company: confidential, secret and top secret. Define which groups of employees are authorized to access what levels and state examples of which documents fall within certain categories and how they should be dealt with, including the protection of information and what punishment will follow in case of breaching such protection.

Having the guts

Forgive me for once again including a story that is hard to believe, but it shouldn't be missing from a chapter on the abuse of authority, and I swear it actually happened. It is not a fabricated story that is here just to make the reading more interesting.

Again, at its core is a bunch of organized employees. This time they **misused their authority in a particularly despicable way**, which I daresay scared a lot of people. I don't think anybody would like to experience this kind of situation, which illustrates how a few individuals who pull together can ruin the good reputation of a company, in this case, an airport.

Place: **Philippines**

Main characters:

Victim no. 1:
airport management

Victims no. 2+:
clients at the airport

×

Employees:
staff working
for airport security

An exotic airport

I'm going to tell you a story that appeared in the news all over the world. I presume that only very few of you, if anyone, runs an airport, but I have decided to tell you this story anyway, as you can learn from it to the benefit of your business future.

A group of security employees working for an airport figured out how they could earn some extra money without actually stealing from their employer. There are countries and regions where it is **much easier to rob customers**, especially if you slightly misuse your facade of power while pretending you are acting in the name of the law.

Vigilant law enforcement

These chaps **took advantage of the law** that specifies that in order to possess a weapon or live ammunition you need a licence, otherwise you're committing a crime. Most of the passengers (probably all of them) had no intention of travelling with illegal weapons or ammunition in their suitcases and yet – surprise, surprise – they were often found in their luggage!

This was the case for a young couple who had decided to travel beyond the bounds of the ordinary – but they certainly hadn't anticipated that they would have such a shocking experience. When, during a security check, a clerk pulled a weapon out of one of their suitcases and a box of ammunition out of another, they couldn't believe their eyes. At first they were taken aback and didn't know how to respond to the situation. They didn't have the slightest idea what would happen next and what to expect. Because of the language barrier they felt even more cornered.

Voluntary bribes

With their poor language skills, they only understood that the **"generous" officers were offering them a way out of trouble**. The surprised and scared travellers **agreed to pay the bribe they were asked for** in exchange for the "friendly" guards not carrying on with the investigation.

They only realized what had probably happened when they were on board the plane. But just like all the other tourists who have had similar experiences, they were just **glad it was all over and they didn't officially complain about the extraordinary experience**. Of course, that meant the airport security staff could continue misusing their position of authority.

So, these cunning employees responsible for airport security checks went on inconspicuously putting ammunition in passengers' luggage, either at check-in or during an X-ray check at security.

If some of the victims had informed airport management about their tricks, other tourists could have been spared this stressful experience and there wouldn't have been any of the bad rumours suggesting that people should stay away from the airport if at all possible.

What is the lesson to be learnt?

What did you think when reading the story above? Was it what I thought – namely, that it is of utmost importance that you develop **a company policy in which:**

- **rules**, including an ethical code, are clearly defined,
- employees are sufficiently **motivated** not to break the rules, and
- any breach of correct conduct will be duly **punished**?

Don't let anyone ruin your company's good name. Clients have a good memory, and they will (or will not) recommend you to their friends and business partners. Good references are essential for the success of your business. Employees who leave a bad impression on your behalf will be forgotten. You won't.

Remember:

- Regularly monitor your company's activity, especially what impression it leaves on customers. Conduct satisfaction surveys: all your customers should have the opportunity to express their opinions and send you their evaluations. It is then up to you what you do with the information.

- Introduce an ethical code of conduct and display it in a visible place so that everyone can see it.
- The further east you go, the less democracy and Western ideology there often is, which results in a steep increase in fishy practices. Don't be indifferent and share your experience with others when you come across something illegal or unpleasant. It may put off others who were considering doing something similar.

A first-class manager

The following story is a textbook example showing that one way to reveal **saboteurs is to promote them**. Do you think it absurd? Then read this story in which an employee's promotion helped reveal the abuse of authority of a top manager working for a German company.

Place: **Germany**

Main characters:

Victim:
the owner
of a big company

Employee:
Helmut,
business director,
later the CEO

Employee of the year

Helmut worked as a business director for a big German company for two years. After that, he had such good references and results that he was promoted and became the CEO. He was on a winning streak. He was obviously very happy, and it was no secret that he was also enjoying life outside his job. No one could overlook the fact that he was living in the lap of luxury.

After Helmut's promotion, the business director vacancy was filled with a new employee whose task it was to take over all Helmut's previous work. In order to quickly find his footing, he thoroughly **researched the former business director's activities**. However, what he found didn't facilitate a smooth start at all.

To tell, or not to tell? That was the question. The new business director had been in place for just a couple of days, and so he wasn't able to accurately estimate how good of a relationship and how much trust there was between Helmut and the company owners. He needed to know whether they would believe a completely new employee if he tried to remove their rose-tinted glasses.

Some extra money

To give you a quick overview, what his previous colleague actually did was nothing short of embezzling assets to the tune of approximately a million dollars! How was Helmut able do it from his position? Simply by electing himself **the only member of a tender committee** that was in charge of countless tenders when selecting the company's business partners.

As you can probably imagine, **the tenders were far from being fair**. Helmut had defined clear conditions that concerned not only commissions, but also some extra remuneration for him.

Fear seals lips

The interesting thing was that some employees later said they had had doubts about Helmut's work and his activities. Several people even admitted they knew about his practices. They never profited from them personally, but **they were afraid to report their superior**.

None of them wanted to be labelled as snitches, while others were aware of Helmut's contacts and they didn't want to get in trouble and risk having to leave the company, so they pretended they didn't know anything, as they didn't have any conclusive evidence anyway. Even though they never benefited from it, **they were afraid to speak up and report their superior**.

There were more reasons why it took so long for Helmut's embezzlement to be revealed. But none of them would have been an issue if the employer had taken certain preventive measures.

What is the lesson to be learnt?

- In this particular case, the employer's reaction was to introduce **an anonymous hotline** through which employees could report anything suspicious without being afraid of being called "informers" or facing any other consequences for their communicativeness. Anonymous hotlines are one of the measures that I strongly recommend you introduce in your company.

- Another aspect that is worth noticing in this story is the "magic" of **tenders**. **Fraud is quite common in this sphere**. It is quite easy for employees who work in positions involving negotiating to help themselves at the expense of their employers. All they need to do is to pick an offer that is not the most advantageous for the company but is more than interesting for the members of the decision-making committee who already have a bribe in their pockets. It should be noted that such practices don't always result in merely a financial loss. Oftentimes they are linked to damage of the owner's or company's good reputation, which may have immense consequences in the future.

Remember:

- Introduce a clear ethical code and zero tolerance for offences.
- Set up an anonymous hotline or suggestion box through which your employees can share their concerns, thoughts and the like.
- Any decision should require the approval of multiple employees. For instance, in case of tenders it should be a selection committee composed of sales managers, an internal customer and maybe even – depending on the situation – a lawyer and a senior manager. Never leave decision making up to a single employee!

IN CONCLUSION

Power is a very dangerous tool. When you're face to face with a person who apparently has control over you, you may feel like David fighting Goliath. Fortunately, we all know what a surprising end that fight had. The fact that you feel disadvantaged at a particular moment doesn't mean that you have no weapons at hand or no means to protect yourself.

It is important to have a company environment that allows anyone to notify you anonymously of what they believe are unfair practices. Whistleblowing is a rather new word in business that is being used more and more often. It is particularly about offering safety to those who are afraid to report anything for fear of losing their jobs.

Chapter X:

Right at the source of temptation – daylight bank robbery

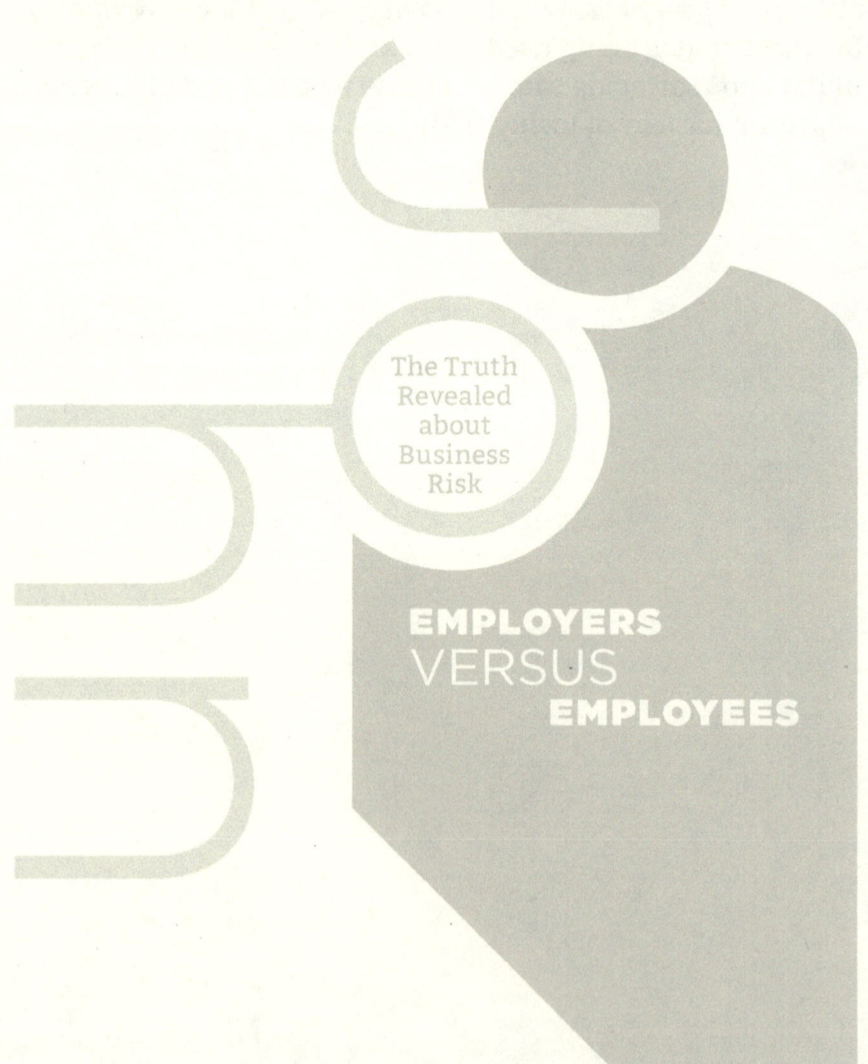

The expression "bank robbery" makes one think of stories from the Wild West, but these days we hardly ever come across the typical robbery that we know from movies.

The banking sector provides fraudsters with specific ways of misusing their positions, and the losses they incur can be really huge. That's why people working for banking institutions should have their ability to resist temptation regularly tested.

Still, there have been a lot of cases where bank employees couldn't curb their appetites. And there are certainly many more to come.

A cash cow

Generally speaking, banks give the impression of being impregnable and absolutely safe institutions full of safety elements and control measures. That's why we entrust them with our money without fear of losing it. In the pursuit of increasing their safety and creditworthiness, they keep making the rules and changes in internal processes stricter and stricter, which chases away any doubts we may have.

However, even banks employ people. People who are duly vetted, trustworthy and hopefully also of moral rectitude, but even such people become insensitive, tired or dissatisfied over the course of time, just like any other employees. And these employees have a big advantage when compared with their clients: they know the weaknesses of their bank from the inside and they are the best-qualified to think up an unobstructed way to commit any kind of fraud or embezzlement.

Place: **Estonia**

Main characters:

Victim:
the owner
and founder of a bank

Employee no. 1:
Kaljo,
a cunning clerk
from the bank's loan
department

Employee no. 2:
Mati,
a waiter in
a nearby restaurant

A powerless fortune maker

Kaljo had spent six years at the counter of the loan department and **he found his job rather dull and monotonous**. True, his decisions on whether to approve or reject loan applications changed customer's lives quite considerably, but he saw nothing more in it than receiving their applications together with all the required documentation and assessing them. He proceeded according to the charts and checked one detail after another to see whether they complied with the bank's requirements. In the end, his computer spat out a result and Kaljo couldn't change anything about it, even if he wanted to.

The worst thing was that he had to listen to the whining of applicants who didn't qualify. He wasn't a social worker, there to calm crying desperate souls and he wasn't interested in hearing sad stories about their lives, even more so because he had no power to change anything. If someone simply didn't meet the requirements, there was nothing Kaljo could do about it.

Originally, he had imagined something else. **He believed he would be able to make life-changing decisions and feel like a powerful man.** In fact, the job was nothing but boring office work, and he had been thinking about a change for quite some time.

A bad starting position

Every day he went for lunch to a restaurant nearby and over all those years he became friends with the staff. Mati worked there as a waiter and both men liked to chat about life every now and then. One day Mati confessed to Kaljo that he was tired of working until late at night and that he would like to have his own place where he could be his own boss and his employees would work night shifts for him instead. But he didn't have enough money to open his own restaurant.

The waiter's income was rather irregular. He had some fixed income, but it was very low and Mati had to earn the rest on tips, or make some extra money at the expense of his employer. As a result, some months were very fruitful, but he couldn't rely on that. Guests came in waves that coincided with the economic situation of the country as well as the "seasons". After pay day the place was full, but the several days leading up to it the restaurant was completely empty and the customers were modest when it came to tips. Moreover, Mati had to pay child support for two kids who, despite never meeting, he had fathered through lack of caution.

That's exactly how he explained everything to Kaljo, who encouraged him not to give up on his dream and to apply for a loan at his bank. **Naturally, regular income, minus financial obligations, was one of the most important parameters**

by which applicants were assessed. When the child support was deducted from Mati's official wages, he was left with almost nothing, so the chances of getting a loan were zero.

A priceless idea

His chances were zero, that is, unless he had a friend who knew the ropes. Kaljo came up with an idea that would sort out Mati's situation while actually profiting both of them. He knew the internal procedures well, how the information submitted was checked. He finally got the chance to help an applicant: he showed the downhearted waiter a way to qualify for the loan.

Mati was told he had to **adjust the income confirmation from his employer** by adding a zero at the end of the amount stated. It was no big lie after all, as he earned much more, so why should he present himself as a poor guy to the bank, he thought. **He followed Kaljo's advice and left the box for stating his obligations blank**. Who cares? He pays money for his children and it's none of the bank's business!

By doing this, his position was much better, as he was viewed as a solvent, low-risk applicant, and after Kaljo approved his application, his bank couldn't disagree. It was clear that this time the computer system would spit out a YES.

A share for the application writer

There was one last thing they had to agree on: remuneration for Kaljo for helping Mati change his life. And Kaljo knew how to handle that smartly. **They increased the amount of the loan Mati applied for by the sum that would go to Kaljo as soon as Mati received the money from the bank**.

Mati believed it was worth it – he knew he would pay more in the end, but he was positive that he could afford it with his future restaurant, the restaurant that he would never have if it weren't for Kaljo. He was so grateful that he didn't question his demand for a rather fat reward.

Everything went as planned. Kaljo entered Mati's details into the computer system and the loan was approved without any objections. The bank paid out the entire sum in a couple of days. Mati sent the promised bonus to Kaljo and bought the restaurant of his dreams. Both parties were satisfied and there was no reason why the bank should check the data retrospectively.

Thwarted plans

But that was soon to change. Mati overestimated his skills and the restaurant didn't run as well as he needed it to. After paying three instalments he lacked the cash for the following month's loan repayment. The season was over, the country was plagued by recession and people preferred to eat home and save money. So, the unavoidable happened. **Mati didn't send the payment in time and the bank started looking into the situation**.

It soon came to light that he didn't provide the bank with accurate information, which meant he had breached the law and **committed loan fraud**. Nobody would have suspected Kaljo of being his accomplice, but Mati broke down during the interrogation and came clean about everything. Checking whether Kaljo actually received the payment was child's play for the bank, so the two of them were soon taken to court.

What is the lesson to be learnt?

- **The most common forms of loan fraud on the part of applicants** are **distorting or concealing information**, which includes not disclosing other expenses and loans. Some studies show that false information appears in about 40 per cent of loan applications. It doesn't matter whether it is distorted or kept secret from the bank intentionally or unintentionally, it is always considered a breach of law.

- Many fraudsters actually get away with cheating like this: if they **duly repay their loan**, the bank has no reason to check on them retrospectively.

- Another favourite trick, when a bank clerk participates in the fraud, is when the applicant puts up as collateral, for instance, diamonds that are nothing more than synthetic imitations or forged artwork and the accomplice from the bank **confirms their genuineness**.

Remember:

- When we take a look at the problem from the bank's perspective, or even that of any other organization, the worst thing is to entrust a single person with decision-making authority. Although it may be more time consuming, you should opt for joint decision making to be on the safe side. We call it the four-eyes principal, and the approval is issued at least by a technical guarantor and an economic guarantor.

- It is also good to set several financial limits for the economic guarantor: for instance, loans of up to 500 dollars can be approved by the assistant, up to 3,000 dollars by the boss and sums exceeding this limit are to be approved exclusively by the department manager and subsequently by the CFO or CEO.

- The genuineness of key documents should be confirmed, for instance, with a notarized copy, not one in which anyone can add a zero as happened in the story above.

Nicholas Leeson

A famous name that shouldn't escape your attention if you want to learn the basics about banks being robbed by their employees is Nicholas Leeson. This chapter would be incomplete without his story. This English gentleman's actions caused the collapse of the UK's oldest merchant bank.

In connection with Leeson, I shall mention another two famous names whom he inspired: Yasuo Hamanaka and John Rusnak committed fraud in the same business and in a similar style.

Place: **United Kingdom**

Main characters:

Victim:
a bank including all its employees

Employee no. 1:
Nicholas Leeson, trader

Employee no. 2:
Jasuo Hamanaka, trader

Employee no. 3:
John Rusnak, trader

An up-and-coming employee

Nicholas Leeson worked as **a stock trader for Barings Bank, the oldest merchant bank** in the UK with more than 200 years of tradition (it existed for precisely 233 years) and whose clients included the Queen.

Ironically, Leeson was originally a very successful trader who did well in his job and everyone, including his employers, predicted that he would have a stellar career. Sadly, later on **he started investing his clients' money, under the name of the bank, in high-risk projects** to a greater extent than he was allowed to, and that was the beginning of the end. Take into account **bad options transactions and zero control mechanisms on the side of the bank** and there you have it, an enormous risk of bankruptcy.

Rogue trader

In a book about his career, *Rogue Trader*, Leeson describes how he ran out of luck after several successful deals, which he tried to disguise with prohibited speculative trades and transactions on behalf of his employer. **However, the losses soon exceeded the total value of the bank's assets**, which resulted in its bankruptcy on 26 February 1995. The bank was later taken over by the Dutch financial company Ing.

Leeson fled but was later caught and sent to prison for six years, of which he served four. During that whole time he didn't once admit that the charges raised against him and the sentence he got were justified. He defended himself by saying that he was pushed to **such risky behaviour by the bank** that kept urging its employees with the appeal: "Make more and more profit!"

Worldwide

A conspicuously similar case has recently occurred in France, where, once again, the person accused is a bank employee. As it is all rather fresh, I don't want to speculate about it. I'll just say that there is still evidence that bank robberies are far from over.

Some other well-known names in connection with this issue, whose cases have been closed, are Yasuo Hamanaka from Japan and John Rusnak from the USA Yasuo Hamanaka is known as **the Copper King**. Behind his employer's back, the Sumitomo Bank, he caused a loss of almost three billion dollars **through unauthorized trading**. John Rusnak caused a loss amounting to "only" seven hundred million dollars.

Some of the losses caused by the rogues mentioned in this story could have been real, but most of them were only artificial, and you can easily imagine in whose pocket the "lost" money ended up.

As you can see, bank robbers are still around, they simply use different methods.

What is the lesson to be learnt?

- This story from the present clearly shows that even though bank robberies are carried out in a different way, they are not a thing of the past. The US Chamber of Commerce revealed that **bank employees in the USA** steal about forty billion dollars a year from their employers. **Compared with pick-pocketing, it is almost nine times more**. The US Chamber of Commerce states that this amount is approximately 1.5 per cent of global trade.

- Another warning message from the story of Nicholas Leeson is that **even a seemingly perfect employee may become risky**, and it is not wise to give up on checking even excellent employees.

- Last but not least, this case teaches us a lesson about how we, as employers, can motivate as well as **demotivate** our employees. It doesn't pay to push too hard.

Remember:

- ▶ Your employees don't necessarily need to work with cash to rob you. Today's world offers many possibilities that were once unimaginable. Not only thanks to globalization, but also because we handle much more money than in the past.
- ▶ Employers should clearly define what employees have the right to access and where they are not allowed.
- ▶ I mentioned rules for setting passwords in Chapter 8. Nevertheless, in the case of bank employees, insurance agents and the like, you should also consider implementing authorization devices such as ID cards with chips where a certificate is stored and only then the access is confirmed by a password.
- ▶ All the operations staff do must be stored in logs with a history of who did what and when.
- ▶ Such employees have to be regularly checked by external auditors.

Identity theft

Statistics confirm that teamwork is generally more successful than the work of an individual. Unfortunately, as you can read in the pages of this book, the same applies to mischievous employees.

You probably expect that the following story will be no exception and that I'm going to tell you something about teamwork again. This time, however, although it concerns bank employees, it is not just about stealing money but also about selling client information.

Place: **Hungary**

Main characters:

Victim no. 1: a bank **Victims no. 2+:** clients	×	**Employees:** inventive bank employees

Phishing

Are you familiar with the term "phishing"? It refers to fraudulent emails that are meant to look like they were sent by your bank or another financial institution. The actual purpose of such emails is to obtain your account log-in details.

You receive a fraudulent email that looks like an official message from the bank where you have account. The content is usually very similar: it seems to be a warning and it's aimed at increasing your protection. Its senders are trying to evoke **panic** in you, the client, by claiming that your money is in great danger unless you respond immediately by clicking on the (phony) link to the bank or financial institution's website and fill in all the required details including your name, the number of your payment card, passwords and so on. Once the thieves have this data, it's a piece of cake for them to rob you.

Identity salespeople

The phishing technique inspired a group of workers at a certain bank. They didn't need to send out fraudulent emails, as they already had **access to all the necessary details**. They knew everything about their clients' identities and their passwords.

They used the data not only to their own benefit, but they also **sold them to other people**. In both cases the result was the same: the clients' money disappeared from their accounts, in small or large sums, or the information was misused for online payments and other purchases.

At the beginning, they only skimmed off small amounts. But they say that the more one has, the more one wants, and that was certainly true in this case. Over the course of time, the employees **completely lost their inhibitions**. They targeted suitable victims and switched from small amounts to rather large sums that were transferred from third parties' accounts to their own accounts that were often located in a different country.

Client awakening

It is obvious that with such blatant carelessness and prodigality, it was just a matter of time before **the aggrieved clients noticed a very considerable decrease in their funds**.

Then things proceeded very quickly and the enterprising gang of employees was finally revealed, convicted and punished accordingly. However, it took rather a long time to completely untangle their network because the transactions involved third parties.

The damage caused was astonishing. Not only did the fraudsters harm an immense number of clients, but naturally also **the bank's reputation**, which had been pristine until then.

What is the lesson to be learnt?

Yet again, we're getting to, although from the other side, the necessity of:

- **control mechanisms,**
- **a company ethical code,**
- **insisting on fair behaviour and**
- **having secure access to all information.**

As in many of the other stories, some of their colleagues suspected that there was something unusual going on, but they didn't have the opportunity or courage to tell: they didn't want to get themselves in trouble as they had no proof.

If the bank had had an **anonymous hotline**, the entire problem could have been revealed much sooner, and the good name of the employer and future of the bank wouldn't have been at stake.

Remember:

▶ The data in the system should never be all in one place and one person should never have access to different kinds of data, meaning that log-in details must be in one system, passwords in another and numbers of payment cards in another.

- The possibility of copying such data from the screen using a simple command (Ctrl+C) should be disabled.
- All employees working for financial institutions should be required to sign an ethical code with clearly defines authority and sanctions – this also applies to any other employees, even outside the banking sector, who work with money.
- Zero tolerance for any kind of rule breach should be adhered to more rigorously in the banking sector than in any other field, and exemplary punishments should be imposed.

A few more inconspicuous accounts

Now I'm going to tell you about a case that became public only rather recently, even though the employees who played the main roles and were undeniably responsible for everything had been cheating their employer for several years. Even in this case, it is surprising that none of the clients noticed anything earlier and that their activities remained unreported. If your money started disappearing, you would tell the bank, wouldn't you?

These employees probably lost their vigilance over the course of time. By taking more and more, they finally drew attention to their actions, and, on top of that, they made front-page news. The media reported that the sum stolen amounted to several millions of dollars. And that is really hard to sweep under the carpet.

Place: **USA**

Main characters:

Victim no. 1: a bank **Victims no. 2+:** clients	**Employees:** several thousand emulous employees

A prestigious banking institution

First, I'd like to say that this story should also serve as a warning to entrepreneurs **not to set employee objectives that are too high – almost unattainable**. It doesn't always end well. Too much pressure was the root of an affair concerning a US bank and its branches.

This prestigious bank with many clients who had entrusted it with their money had a clearly defined **motivational bonus programme**. In order to qualify for the bonuses, employees had to meet several conditions. The fundamental one was **winning new clients**. In reality, the actual aim was to gather more money, not clients, which, I think, doesn't require a more profound explanation.

Fictitious accounts

As you simply cannot meet potential clients at every stage, the employees who wanted to get the bonuses went about it quite cunningly. They chose several existing clients and opened **new fictitious bank accounts** for them **without letting them know**, to which they transferred money from their current accounts.

Naturally, **the relevant banking fees were charged to the clients** and **payment cards** were issued for all the fake accounts.

The fake unauthorized accounts lived their own lives and the illusion around them was perfect: the bank employees even linked them to fake email addresses that served for frequent communication between the bank and fictitious clones of the real clients. They left nothing to chance in case someone from management started looking closely into these clients.

At first sight, there didn't seem to be anything wrong with it. It was a public secret among the employees of various branches scattered all over the USA. There was a kind of a secret unwritten confidentiality agreement between them.

Thanks to this cohesion, the employees qualified for the coveted bonuses without being suspected of anything, while their employer was delighted by how the bank, already a giant, kept growing.

Accounts in the red

As I've written before, the employees probably **slackened their vigilance** after the scam had worked for so long. Or was it because it was meant to happen? Maybe it was just a simple confirmation of the well-known saying "The pitcher goes so often to the well that it is broken at last!"

Anyway, there was a moment when the first warning sign was sent from the bank to some of its clients suggesting there was something wrong. The clients who received the message were scared stiff. The **careless machinations** of bank clerks that had included money transfers between real and fictitious accounts led to a situation where there was surprisingly little money in the real clients' accounts. Some people were in an even worse situation: they were in the red and the bank had asked them to pay a fee for being overdrawn.

Of course, the clients were far from tolerating – they were not staying home and weeping into their pillows. Most of them either called the bank or went to the bank in person. They were astonished when they realized what had happened. Most of them couldn't understand how they hadn't noticed that **someone else was managing their money their own way**. They could hardly believe that there were other bank accounts under their names. As they hadn't opened them themselves, there were no contracts. They hadn't signed anything, hadn't deposited any money and had never made a single transfer.

Millions of dollars

The outraged clients refused to come accept the situation. The Consumer Financial Protection Bureau (CFPB) intervened and the following investigation revealed that two and half million dollars had been withdrawn from the legitimate accounts.

The case is still under investigation as I write these lines. **So far, the bank has sacked 5,300 employees** who were probably connected with the scam. Time will tell what the final consequences for them will be.

Even the bank was partly to blame as it **couldn't deny that it had no supervision over its employees**, so it had to pay its dues. It is said that the fine, amounting to **a hundred million dollars**, was the highest imposed by the CFPB in the past five years. But it didn't end there.

The bank was, quite logically, afraid of a mass exodus of its clients and tried to offset the loss of client confidence by sending them financial compensation. According to the available resources, they were offered **compensation totalling five million dollars**.

The motivational programme really got out of the employer's hands this time.

What is the lesson to be learnt?

The conclusions that can be drawn from the story are rather obvious:

- The employer lost a considerable amount of money, prestige and client confidence that had taken many years to build.
- Clients left the bank on a mass scale and they **didn't spare the bank the disservice of negative advertising**. That's no surprise after what they had been through.
- The clients who stayed with the bank **had, naturally, a lot of doubts** and it is not certain whether they will remain loyal to the bank in the future.
- With respect to the situation, the bank can forget about attracting new clients any time soon. **Its shares have decreased dramatically** and its future is uncertain.

I can only speculate whether all of this would have happened if the employees hadn't been under so much pressure and **the amount of their salaries hadn't been conditioned by meeting objectives under a badly defined motivational programme**. We'll never learn that.

Another parlous aspect was the **fatal failure of the employer's control**. One would have not expected such bad oversight at the third largest US bank.

Naturally, there are many theories about what the reality was. Some people even **suspect that the bank's management knew about the scam** or at least suspected there was something wrong while tolerating it. But these are only theories that will either be confirmed or disproved by further investigation.

Remember:

- Winston Churchill said: "The only statistics you can trust are those you falsified yourself". What did he mean by that? That the objectives defined for employees should be realistic and that there is no such thing as endless growth. Every day I come across employees who, in a chase to meet unrealistic targets, give a slant to their performance in various ways, be it data about their clients, numbers of accounts or business results. This concerns every field of business and may severely damage your good reputation.
- Carefully check all the data you're presented with.
- Use external advisors and auditors to help you reveal any manipulations.

IN CONCLUSION

A bank should be synonymous with security. You entrust it with your money because you don't want to lose it. Unfortunately, even at banks there can be employees with weaknesses, problems and bad character traits, so the risk with them is the same as with any other employees.

However, it should be noted that the scam doesn't have to be about manipulating cash. Today's digital world gives thieves many more opportunities. What suffered the greatest damage was the bank's reputation. It may take years for you to build up a good reputation and then your employees can destroy it in a single season and push you to the brink of bankruptcy.

Whatever field you do business in, you should know that appearances can be deceiving and that no matter how safe you think the environment is, the darkest place is always under the candle's flame. There's never enough cautiousness to spare and thorough supervision is always appropriate.

Chapter XI:

Sticking your neck out – damaged reputation

There have been many stories in this book about how employers' good names were damaged. Still, or maybe because of that, I've decided to write an entire chapter on the subject.

It doesn't matter what kind of business you are involved in or whether you employ hundreds of employees or just one, as an employer it is actually you who puts your head above the parapet every time an employee acts on your behalf.

Even if your employees aren't cheating or tricking you specifically, their actions can still be seriously detrimental to you. The following stories that I have come across over the years will show you how.

Gambling with love

I've mentioned data abuse on several occasions. People still generally think that such abuse primarily concerns IT companies and that attacks usually come from the outside.

That's why I have decided to tell you a story from a different field. Notice that the one who misuses the data is an employee. The consequences for the owner were very serious in this case, as the loss of reputation destroyed the business.

Place: **Austria**

Main characters:

Victim no. 1:
owner of a dating agency

Victims no. 2+:
Hilda and other clients

Employee:
Irma,
a persuasive assistant
and a matchmaker

Desire for love

If life circumstances lead you to a dating agency, you may think that the worst thing that could happen to you is that you could be offered a disgusting, unsuitable date.

That's what Hilda thought, too. She was fifty and quite a successful woman. She wasn't short of money, she enjoyed her job and lived a happy life. Then there came a moment in her life when she realized that she didn't want to be alone anymore.

For such a well-situated lady, it would be somewhat inappropriate to look for acquaintances at bars, she thought. She wouldn't be interested in men who were on the prowl at such places anyway. And she couldn't find anyone in her circles. So, after thorough consideration she decided to **use the services of a discreet dating agency**.

When she arrived at the first meeting with an assistant, Irma, who was to write down all her requirements and enter the information about their new client in the database, Hilda was pleasantly surprised and all her initial doubts soon disappeared. She had made a good choice. Irma was the nicest lady Hilda had met over the past couple of months, **and so she wasn't afraid to tell her almost everything about herself**.

First dates

In a couple of days, Hilda started receiving offers for dates. She was happy with the selection of suitors. All of them were well-situated, just like her. She met a few of them in a café, but every date ended up being just a friendly conversation over a cup of coffee. There was no chemistry, but the agency certainly wasn't to be blamed for that. After some time, Hilda eventually met one gentleman who she was attracted to and they started dating.

All of this could have ended with Hilda and her partner romantically walking off hand in hand into the sunset. I wish. Life writes more prosaic stories sometimes, which Hilda was soon to find out in a rather disagreeable way.

Hilda for sale

After some time, Hilda started to get more email spam than ever. Her new partner was having the same experience, so they just complained to each other about the insolence and methods of some businesses.

They received phone calls with offers for various investments and although Hilda refused all of them, her mobile phone usually rang several times a day. When she complained about the unsolicited calls to her partner in the evening, they found out that he was receiving the same offers at the same time.

This could be no coincidence. Hilda decided to contact one of the companies that regularly filled her inbox with "irresistible offers". She met the boss in person and when she put pressure on him, he told her that he had **bought her personal data from the agency** that she had used to find her life partner.

Sensitive data on a silver platter

Hilda contacted the other men she had met through the agency and she wasn't surprised to find out that all of them were facing the same problem.

Together, they succeeded in proving that Irma had **sold on their personal data**. Their names, phone numbers, addresses, emails, hobbies, interests and even their bank account numbers – everything that could be considered confidential and was of any value.

The agency owner **dismissed Irma and apologized to the clients**, but that was not the end. The negative advertising stirred up by the affair **put an end to the agency**. No prospective clients wanted to be a part of anything with such a bad reputation. The word “discrete” in the logo of the dating agency suddenly seemed like a joke.

What is the lesson to be learnt?

- The story shows that the aggrieved ones in this case **were not only the clients**. There was an aftermath, and the reputation that **suffered the most damage** was that of the agency and its **owner**.

- If your business rises and falls with how well you work with people and their trust, **keeping their data secure should be your top priority**. Lost confidence is hard to win back and even when you dismiss and punish the culprit, it still might not return.

- **Preventive measures** for such cases are as follows:
  1. focus on **selecting honest employees** and **educating them** through special training on how to handle confidential information,
  2. **use** appropriate **technology** that will prevent data leakage and disable their abuse and
  3. have a clear **response and solution plan** in case anything happens and inform your employees of the **consequences** they will face if they break the rules.

Remember:

- You must always carefully protect client data from abuse, otherwise you will have a problem with the law!
- You should grant access to personal data to only a limited number of employees with clearly defined authorization who have been trained and go through regular checks.
- Inform your clients of their rights and what kind of services they can count on from your company (what you guarantee them).

Holidays not worth a brass farthing

The leitmotif that connects this story with the previous one is an unusual perspective on how data can be misused, although it occurred in a completely different environment: a car rental service on an Italian island.

In this case as well, the people who suffered the most harm were not the clients who were robbed, but the company owner whose reputation suffered. It is never good advertising for a business, and it is really hard to repair a damaged reputation.

Place: **Italy**

Main characters:

Victim no. 1: Luigi, the owner of a car rental service	×	**Employee:** Antonio, employee of a car rental service
Victims no. 2+: clients		

A holiday (auto)dream

In summer, a lot of people fly to sunny seaside resorts. But what do they do there? Is everyone happy spending the entire time in a single spot, on one beach, next to one pool? Those who like to travel around the destination turn to **car and bike rentals**.

This is exactly what one family did during their holiday on the picturesque Italian island of Sardinia. Immediately after their arrival, they went into a car rental office at the airport that caught their attention with favourable prices. The man who helped them was Antonio. They will certainly remember his name for many years to come, trust me.

The car rental company belonged to Luigi, an entrepreneur who spent most of his time on the Italian mainland where he ran a network of car rental offices all year round. He also had several rental branches on islands, but those were only open during the peak season, and he considered them a seasonal bonus. He always hired two employees for each of his island rental offices to take care of the business for those couple of months.

So, the family rented a car, paid and, in case they had an accident, damaged the car or didn't refill the tank before returning it, they provided Antonio **with their payment card details** as security. It is a rather common practice, they had done so before in other countries and islands and they didn't think anything of it.

Even money travels

A cloud appeared in the sky above their serene holiday, when one of the parents just happened to check, out of sheer boredom, their bank account balance. What a shock it was when they found out that they had been charged for the car twice!

As they had rented the car for many days, the sum wasn't exactly negligible: almost 600 euros had been deducted from the account without their consent and, apparently, it had gone to a different Italian account than the first payment.

Revelation

Their shock soon turned into anger and they stepped into action. Antonio was frankly taken aback. Most of the customers didn't actually discover his trick with the double payment and "small tip" that he withdrew from their accounts until after they returned home, if ever.

Since tourists generally rented cars for only a few days, **the sums were usually lower** and remained unnoticed or were believed to be just one of the many payments made on the holiday. Even those who tried hard to recall what that payment was for eventually waved it off and **decided not to worry about it anymore**.

Those who noticed the odd payment during their holiday were often deterred by the **language barrier**, as Antonio persistently only spoke Italian and didn't respond to English. Others **were put off by the paperwork** and the trouble linked with investigating the circumstances of the case.

So Antonio got away with **misusing cards and temporary identity theft** for quite a long time, although it was often a close escape. True, it sometimes happened that a careful and knowledgeable client blocked the extra payment, but those were the only times Antonio got into hot water.

One rotten apple can spoil the whole barrel

As soon as this case came to light, other deceived clients called in. There were more and more accusations. The name of the car rental service and its owner were more and more frequently mentioned in connection with scams, thefts and dishonest conduct.

It affected the entire company including its branches on the peninsula where no one knew Antonio or had ever heard of him and customers were always treated fairly. It is true what they say: one rotten apple can spoil the whole barrel.

What is the lesson to be learnt?

- By telling you this story I wanted to draw your attention to the fact that data theft and their abuse **may take different forms**.

- But if you let **your employees** harm YOUR clients, customers and business partners, **it is your problem**.

- I have deliberately written "YOUR clients, customers and

business partners" as **it is you whose reputation gets damaged** and whose livelihood may be put in jeopardy.

Remember:

- Don't forget to train your employees thoroughly.
- Again, I remind you that there should be zero tolerance and that any wrongdoing should be punished.
- It also matters how clearly you state what the customer is entitled to and how well you describe the services and guarantees that you offer.
- In addition to prevention, thorough supervision of all branches and detached departments is also important. Random unannounced checks and mystery shoppers will save you from having to cope with unpleasant surprises later on.

A lucky chimney sweep

Sadly, the main victim of the following story is an elderly gentleman who was dependent on other people's help. That's why he made use of certain services he was offered.

He suffered the consequences and had an unpleasant experience. He's definitely not going to say anything good about any of the companies involved. I presume you'll understand when you have read the story.

Place: **Czech Republic**

Main characters:

Victim no. 1: the owner of a care service agency	**Employee no. 1:** Jiřina, an inventive carer
Victim no. 2: the owner of a company that sweeps and inspects chimneys	**Employee no. 2:** Oldřich, a completely independent chimney sweep
Victim no. 3: Václav, an elderly client	

In need of help

Václav was eighty-five and lived completely on his own. After a hip surgery, he had to admit that he hadn't got back into the shape he'd been in before. Even though his two children tried to help, they couldn't provide him with the care he needed. His son Vašek and daughter Renata were grown-up. They had their own families, jobs and duties, and they simply couldn't take care of him twenty-four/seven.

Renata offered to have him move into their place, at least until he recovered, but her dad turned it down. He liked his privacy and he liked to believe that he could still manage everything by himself despite his advanced age. He had lived all his life in his small brick house, and all his memories were tied to it. Although he knew that he should probably accept his daughter's offer, he insisted on his "No". Maybe he was worried that he might not return to his home ever again.

Before he broke his hip, when he took a hard fall on some black ice, Václav had been self-sufficient. He could do the shopping and cook for himself, and he was able to visit the doctor without anyone's assistance. But suddenly, he had to admit that **he was going to need help**.

Jiřina, a guardian angel

Renata and Vašek put their heads together and decided that they would find **a carer for their pig-headed father**. They researched, read through the references of various care service agencies and eventually picked one that had very good reviews.

The carer they chose was a thirty-eight-year-old woman named Jiřina. She and Václav soon grew fond of each other. She was a hearty woman who wasn't afraid of work, and she ignored the old man's grumbles and unwillingness to cooperate. In fact, she succeeded in straightening him out: she made him do all the necessary rehabilitation exercises, she helped him overcome his initial shyness when she helped with personal hygiene, she did some shopping for him, picked up lunches for him, kept an eye on his medication and was there to help any time he needed it.

No wonder their relationship **soon turned into a friendship**. Jiřina was like a guardian angel to Václav. After a couple of months, he considered that slender energetic woman who was the same age as his daughter almost a member of the family. **He had complete faith in her**.

A chimney sweep comes into the picture

Days went by and Václav appreciated **how beneficial Jiřina's care was for him** – he was feeling better and better. He got involved in some housework and he could finally walk again. As he started moving around to rooms of the house where he hadn't been for some time, he decided to heat up his entire house.

When trying to make his house warmer and cosier, he realized that the secondary stove in the house was fuming too much. The room was still full of smoke that had moved through the house to the front door, when the bell suddenly rang. It was Jiřina, who had arrived just in time. Just like a guardian angel, she knew what to do. **She pulled out the phone number of a chimney sweep** who she claimed was the best in the world.

Václav was grateful for that and he immediately called Oldřich, the chimney sweep in question. On the phone, Oldřich sounded like a professional with a friendly approach. Since Václav mentioned that he had got his number from their "mutual friend", Oldřich was very forthcoming and offered to come quite soon.

Václav looked at his calendar. He had to refuse the first date offered as he had an appointment at the hospital that day. It was in the next town and Václav knew from previous experience that it would take him almost the whole day. Václav didn't want Oldřich to think he was fussy, so he explained everything in rather great detail. Fortunately, Oldřich understood, so they found another date.

A different kind of hospital visit

The night before the appointment, Václav called his son Vašek to make sure that he hadn't forgotten about it and that he'd take him there as they'd arranged. Jiřina had the day off and it actually wasn't her job to drive her client everywhere. But Vašek was surprised by Vaclav's call and they argued about which date they'd agreed on. They decided to call the hospital where they confirmed that Václav's appointment was actually fixed for the following week.

So Václav stayed home, despite his calendar indicating an appointment. It was to be a day just like any other, only without Jiřina. And, as he wasn't expecting anybody, he was very surprised to hear a key in the front door in the middle of the afternoon. He stood up and went warily to the doorway.

There he met an uninvited guest who was just as surprised as he was. It was a **man that Václav had never seen before and yet he had keys to his house**. But the worst was still to come. The unfamiliar man panicked and pushed the owner of the house so hard that he fell and hit his head on the edge of a chest of drawers. He was lying on the floor, blood trickling from his head.

The uninvited guest didn't care about that. He had a different mission: he went to the living room and Václav could only listen to him rummaging around. Unable to stand, Václav was lying helplessly in the doorway when he saw the man walking away with his booty.

The most important item was a seemingly ordinary **shoe box where Václav kept his savings**. He didn't trust banks, the nearest cash machine was in town where he hardly ever went and only his family knew about his cache. He had never thought that anybody else would be able to sniff it out. Václav fainted.

When he came to his senses, he was alone in the house. Mustering all his strength he crawled to the phone and called his daughter. She arrived immediately, followed by an ambulance. Václav actually did have to go to hospital that day after all.

Solving the mystery

Of course, the police started investigating the case: a mugged elderly man was no triviality. It came out that Václav had discreetly managed to save around 6,000 Czech crowns, some 200 euros.

The police solved the mystery quickly, although Václav and his children weren't happy to hear their conclusions. Jiřina, the guardian angel, had come up with a sophisticated burglary plan after winning Václav's confidence. That uninvited guest who had come to Václav's house with the keys was her partner Oldřich who had a rather dishonourable history.

He got a copy of the keys from Jiřina. It was no problem for her. In fact, if she had asked, trusting Václav would have even given her his own. But that would have made her a prime suspect, and she didn't want that. In addition to the keys, Jiřina gave Oldřich a detailed description of the house, where he could find what and, most importantly, where the old man kept his money.

Then all he needed to do was to wait for a moment when nobody was at home. If Václav hadn't confused the date of his appointment, Oldřich could have burgled his flat unhindered. Unfortunately, the two of them met, which was a bad surprise for both of them. The chimney sweep didn't bring luck to anyone that day.

What is the lesson to be learnt?

- Undoubtedly, neither of the two employees served their employer well. The care service agency as well as the chimney sweeping company bore the consequences of the mischievous couple. **Their reputations suffered greatly**, although **the owner of the chimney sweeping company** got entangled by sheer chance and there was nothing he could have done as his employee received the order through his private phone: **no preventive measures would have been effective anyway**.

- I see a very big mistake in how **the care service agency vetted its employees**. In fields like this, employers **should be extremely careful about the quality as well as the safety** of the services they offer. It is impossible to run such a business without clients.

- I also recommend **checking your employees' pasts** and if you decide to hire someone who is in someone else's "bad books" (has a criminal record), you should watch them extra carefully.

Remember:

- ▶ Make sure your employees don't have criminal records and look into their history and references from previous jobs.
- ▶ When you offer services, regularly conduct customer satisfaction surveys.
- ▶ Establish a hotline through which your clients can inform you of any doubts they may have about the quality of your services.

Custom-made babies

Even the most serious-looking employees working in top positions at institutions that are meant to help people can actually irreparably damage your company's reputation and shock the whole world. All it takes is for them to follow their own interests, in addition to yours, while enjoying almost limitless powers.

They could certainly tell you such stories at a fertility clinic in Belgium. The clinic helped many desperate couples make their dreams come true by assisting them to bring a child into the world. However, after some years it proved that things might be quite different than expected.

Place: **Belgium**

Main characters:

Victim no. 1: owner of a fertility clinic **Victims no. 2+:** a couple who couldn't have children	**Employee:** Marcel, director of a fertility clinic

Where nature fails, man helps

Having children is one of the most natural human needs. Although there are people who don't want kids, there are more and more people for whom this wish has become the most important thing in life, and yet it seems impossible for them to conceive. The number of infertile people (mainly men) is growing for many different reasons, so many couples cannot have a baby the natural way.

With the latest scientific and medical advances, there are more and more **specialized places where people give nature a helping hand**. They can replace a low-quality embryo or sperm with biological material from a donor, implant a fertilized egg in a surrogate mother and save premature babies born at extremely low birth weights. Despite discussions about how unnatural such interventions are, childless couples see them as **miracles and are immensely grateful for the accomplishments of modern medicine**.

A baby that meets your specifications

There were hundreds of satisfied clients of this particular Belgian fertility clinic. Marcel, an empathetic, good-humoured, middle-aged director had been running it for two decades. During consultations, he lifted a heavy burden from many couples, because he was able to make them believe that **he would help them to soon have the greatest baby they could ever imagine**.

He worked particularly with couples that needed sperm from donors. He advised them how to correctly set the criteria for their selection, what aspects they could "order" in advance. He needed to persuade most clients to adjust their ideas of what their child should be like so that the donor would match them in terms of their occupation or education, their interests, talents and physical appearance **so that the child wouldn't differ from the parents at first sight**.

The power of genetics

All parents think that they have the most beautiful baby in the world. That is doubly true for the parents of babies born after many years of unsuccessful attempts and considerable financial and emotional investment, who wished so desperately for them. And, of course, everybody who sees a newborn baby voices an opinion on who the baby takes after.

Friends who know that half of the couple's biological material had to be replaced with someone else's naturally tend to avoid such topics. However, **genetics is sometimes merciless**, as a young gentleman was shocked to discover when he looked in the mirror one day and realized who he actually looked like. **And that person certainly wasn't his father**.

This young man looked exactly like Marcel, a man who his family went to see each year at Christmastime with small gifts. So he'd actually met his mirror-image in person several times.

When he told his parents what he thought, they agreed that **they'd had the same suspicion for some time but were reluctant to admit it to themselves**. According to their selection criteria, the donor was to have been a tall blue-eyed blond man, just like his father who had brought him up, but their son was the only one in the family who had brown eyes and brown hair.

Father, come clean

When they approached Marcel and asked whether there could have been any mistake, he laughed at the very thought of it. But there was a strange tinge of satisfaction in his look, so the family took it further. **In addition to informing the clinic's management about their suspicion, they also contacted the media and unleashed hell**.

Over a couple of weeks, the clinic was contacted by dozens of families who thought that **the biological father of their children was Marcel**. Their children were far from the criteria they had specified for the donors, while they all had very similar features.

Marcel was suddenly under great pressure and there was only one way he could disprove the allegations: with **DNA testing**. However, **he refused to undergo testing** insisting that he'd done nothing wrong. If the allegations were proved true, it would mean that Marcel, in addition to misleading clients, had broken another rule that stipulated **that one donor could only be the father of up to six children**.

One big family

The shameful allegations didn't only concern Marcel, but also had an impact on his family. Eventually, **his own son decided to give his DNA** and tests showed **a family relationship match with at least twenty children**.

Marcel was immediately deprived of his office, but before there could be a trial, he died of a heart attack. Nobody will ever find out **what exactly led him to replace the donors' sperm with his own**, thus fathering dozens of offspring. At present, there are sixty cases where his fatherhood is suspected!

You certainly know why I'm telling you this story in the chapter on damaging employers' reputations. Would you go to such a fertility clinic to pick a donor for your dream baby? Probably not, just as would be the case with many other couples who are in such a situation.

The clinic lost the confidence of many of its potential clients and the general public in such a bizarre manner that its owner is unlikely to be able to save it from going under.

What is the lesson to be learnt?

- **We don't know what the scammer's motive was in this case**, so we can only guess whether it was excessive male ego and the belief that he was the best male in the world, or whether he just enjoyed being able to play with destiny.

- How was it that he could get away with this trick for so many years? Obviously, the clinic didn't **correctly set protective measures and control mechanisms** concerning the samples taken.

- **The loss of confidence** will probably prove **fatal** in this case: it was covered in the media and the scandal reverberated internationally.

Remember:

- You can make up for lost profit or a project in the red, but a damaged reputation is something that may ruin you for many years to come. Defining control mechanisms, the four-eye rule and the regular rotation of employees with similar jobs should safeguard that your process will not be interfered with, neither due to a set-up error, nor purposefully by an offender.

- Sometimes, a mere work rut can be the trigger. Try to offer your employees open dialogue, as it often leads to changes and improvement. Don't oppress them and listen to when they have to say about innovating your processes.

- A lot has been written in this book about selecting employees, but trust me, not everyone proceeds and behaves as you would expect them to or the same way that you would. In our society, the multicultural environment is often promoted, but what is normal for us may be forbidden for some other people and vice versa. Therefore, you should be careful and double check your employees' conduct and their attitude to your company's values.

- Hold regular training sessions on principles of conduct and adherence to the values and visions you've defined.

IN CONCLUSION

These stories were meant to show you that, regardless of your field of business, your employees are the face of your company and selecting the right ones is of primordial importance.

If even the bottommost shop assistant frowns at your customers, it may be the reason why they stop buying from you. They don't know her name and they don't care what it is. But you're the one who put her in the position, so you're responsible for ensuring that customers are served as if you yourself were attending to them.

Chapter XII:

An eye for an eye – former employees

In this book I have mentioned many kinds of high-risk employees and how they may conduct themselves, but there is one extremely high-risk group that I haven't mentioned yet. Not because I consider them less dangerous, quite the contrary. They can be very dangerous, because their actions are driven by emotions such as anger, hatred and a desire for vengeance.

People you have shown your mistrust of by dismissing them from a cushy job and bringing their regular income to a halt. The offenders in this chapter are former employees taking revenge.

The case of the lost cash box

There are unpredictable problems with employees from time to time. Even when they are ex-employees. If they decide to harm you, you don't have many options at hand to prevent them from doing so, unless you took preventive measures while they were working for you. The following stories are meant to motivate you to implement such measures.

Place: **Germany**

Main characters:

Victim: Theobald, owner of a shop	**Former employee**: Oliver, storeroom assistant

Village shops

Theobald owned several grocery stores. They were located in small picturesque villages far from bigger towns. The inhabitants of the villages were happy to have a shop nearby as it made their lives easier and more pleasant. Moreover, Theobald employed several local people, who didn't have to commute dozens of miles to work, so the shops benefited all.

The local people always tried to accommodate their neighbours' needs, so they were in charge of ordering the goods and the customers were happy to buy from them. Theobald kept an eye on everything, he took care of the invoices and administration and the shops ran like clockwork without too much stress.

Naturally, there were some employees every now and then who weren't good for the business or weren't reliable. Such things cannot be avoided in business, so Theobald didn't worry much about it. All new employees signed contracts with a probation period, and if it came out during that period that they were not up to his standards, Theobald dismissed them without any hard feelings.

To find a replacement in a small village where work opportunities were rather scarce was not difficult. Theobald knew that people come and go, so he didn't think much of it when he fired twenty-five-year-old Oliver after he had performed terribly for two months.

Auntie's intervention

He already felt a little unsure about Oliver when he hired him. But he needed someone to stock goods and Ingrid, who had worked for him for ten years and had always been great, couldn't do it herself. When she recommended her nephew Oliver to Theobald, he considered it a guarantee of high-quality.

However, after a couple of weeks he found out that the young lad **wasn't exactly keen on work**. What was worse, he counted on the fact that his aunt would never complain about him. So, Ingrid **did all the work herself** and Oliver rubbed his hands together, satisfied with how he'd arranged everything.

The village grapevine

But village tam-tams are a great tool for communication. Word spreads fast, often even beyond the village, so the news even got to Theo. As soon as he found out how things stood, he sacked Oliver and hired Hugo, a serious-looking man in his thirties, to do the job. The only confusion caused by the change concerned **the keys to the shop and storeroom**: they didn't have the right number.

Ingrid didn't want her boss to have to deal with any more trouble. She felt responsible for the fiasco with Oliver's work ethics, and she promised she would look after her new colleague and show him the ropes. She gave Hugo a spare bunch of keys saying she'd look for the missing keys when she had time. She must have put them aside somewhere, it was impossible that she could have lost them as she always guarded them zealously.

Mysterious disappearance of the cash box

It became apparent that the keys actually weren't lost some ten days later when **the cash box** disappeared from the shop. Ingrid didn't notice it at first: she arrived at work as usual, opened the shop, switched the lights on, arranged some goods on the shelves, made coffee, turned the sign on the door to "Open" and stood at the cash register.

Only then did she bend over to pull out the box with the money from underneath. As there was no bank in the vicinity, Theobald had arranged with her, just as with all the other shop assistants in his village grocery stores, that he would always pick up the cash in person on certain days. It had worked just fine since people in small villages are something like a big family. Everybody knows about everything and nobody expects to be robbed by the locals.

But that day Ingrid was rooted to the spot when she couldn't find the cash box. When Hugo showed up, she questioned him. He objected vehemently against her suspicion and insisted that she call the owner and the police. Nobody could understand **how anyone could get into a locked shop** and carry away a cash box without raising suspicion or damaging the lock. Only when Ingrid remembered the lost keys did everything start to make sense.

Return of the villain nephew

Oliver, after getting the sack, couldn't be bothered with returning the keys. When he was leaving, he knew he'd come back for the cash box one day. And he did, as he'd planned, except he didn't expect to get caught.

What is the lesson to be learnt?

- Even if you feel that there's a family atmosphere in your company and your employees trust one another, **don't forget to safeguard your property**.

- **Don't hire** new employees **based only on recommendations** from their relatives or your current employees and vet everyone thoroughly.

- Have them **sign a protocol** defining what they've received from you and make it part of their employment contract. When they leave your company, insist that they return everything.

- Don't assign tasks to employees who are not **competent** for the given task **or duly trained**.

Remember:

- As I've mentioned before, the worst thing you can do is to give a job to one of your relatives, because then you're often expected to turn a blind eye. But that's exactly what you shouldn't do: because of your other employees, if for no other reason. Everyone must play by the same rules.

- Your employment contracts should always stipulate the material liability of those employees who handle your property or cash.

- Make sure you have appropriate safety measures in place, not only in terms of changing the locks every time a key gets lost, but also in terms of changing the passwords to your security system, IT system and so on.

Fictitious booking

Employment contracts are terminated day in and day out. So dismissing an employee is nothing that requires special attention. An exception may be when **a frustrated employee is dismissed** with stress on the word "frustrated".

Such former employees can often turn into vengeance on two legs. It is almost admirable how much energy and time some people can spend devising and implementing plans that aim to complicate your life somehow. It makes one think that if they had exerted so much effort in their work, they might never have been sacked.

Place: **United Kingdom**

Main characters:

Victims: Ryan a Emma, owners of a hotel	×	**Former employee**: Lucas, receptionist

A useless receptionist

Lucas was a failure as a receptionist. Guests and even colleagues **complained about him all the time**. Lucas arrived late to work, or sometimes not at all. He often smelled of alcohol, looked scruffy and when he wasn't being rude to guests, he just ignored them.

He didn't complete his tasks. His colleagues had to do his work for him so that the hotel could continue to operate as usual. They were fed up with him. At first, they felt sorry for him, as he was going through a tough time after a break up with his girlfriend. They helped cover his butt out of loyalty so that the bosses wouldn't find out. But when the situation didn't improve, rather to the contrary, they decided they wouldn't hold their tongues any longer.

An uncompromising notice

The bosses started receiving complaints about Lucas from his colleagues, in addition to those filed by guests. No wonder Ryan and Emma were soon fed up with him.

They'd worked hard for so many years before they could afford to buy their own little hotel. They'd been running it for hardly a year and the last thing they needed were negative reviews from dissatisfied guests, especially when their hotel was rarely full.

So **they bid farewell** to the rude receptionist rather quickly. Nobody wants negative advertising and having such a weak link in the team would definitely result in that very soon.

Incredibly high demand for accommodation

As if by magic, after Lucas left, there was an incredible increase in requests for accommodation. Emma, who was the main person responsible for the new online bookings system, was over the moon: Ryan will finally understand that a modern hotel cannot make do with just a phone, she thought!

There were so many people booking accommodation online **that the hotel had to turn away some customers**. That's exactly what its owners had dreamt of! A cosy family hotel with a friendly atmosphere that guests would queue for!

Initial doubts

The first doubts arose when Emma **mistakenly confirmed an online reservation for a room that Ryan had just booked for a client on the phone**. Emma had to get in touch with "her" customer in order to offer him another vacancy. But she received no reply to her email or text message, the phone number was disconnected.

Emma found it **strange**. She tried to contact another client who had booked a room online. She was relieved when he answered the call. But then she felt miserable again when he told her that he hadn't booked anything, he didn't intend to travel anywhere and he'd actually never even heard of their hotel. That was too much for Emma to take.

She took the list and together with Ryan tried to contact everyone who had a booking with them. **Only about a tenth of the bookings were genuine**. It was one of two scenarios with the remainder: either the people called had no idea that a room was booked on their behalf or none of the contact details worked.

The ex-receptionist's move

The hotel owners soon got to the bottom of it. They found out that it was Lucas who was behind the whole thing. Their ex-receptionist was so frustrated that **he decided to harm their business** as much as he believed that they'd hurt him by dismissing him.

He had just gone through a break up and nobody had taken his difficult personal situation into consideration! There was no gain in it for him, except for the pleasure of getting revenge.

What is the lesson to be learnt?

- Trouble-making employees who have issues with some addiction (drinking, gambling, drugs, for example) can be dangerous even after they're fired. They can surprise you with a sudden strike of inventiveness. It is these sorts of people who blame others for their failures, never themselves. **Be cautious and vigilant**.

- There have even been extreme cases where ex-employees felt they were so wronged that **they resorted to violence against ex-employers, and sometimes they even considered murder**. I know, it is hard to believe, but we shouldn't close our eyes to it. Such things actually happen and, sadly, they don't always have a happy ending.

- Your current and former employees aside, there is another angle this problem can be viewed from. If your business receives inquiries in several ways, you should always **check the credibility of the client placing the order** and you should keep in mind that when you accept the order, a new contractual/business relationship begins with obligations for both parties. Saying more would get us too far off the topic of employers and their employees.

Remember:

- When dismissing a troublemaker, it pays to use the services of a psychologist who can settle the situation with such a person in an expert manner. You should always try to part ways "amicably".

- Explain to the employee why you are dismissing him or her and ask for his or her "consent", by saying, for instance, "If you were in my shoes, wouldn't you do the same?" or "Do you agree that when someone doesn't show up at work, they are not entitled to wages?" and the like.

- Sometimes it is necessary to deal with a situation at the onset so that it doesn't turn ugly and motivate the employee to take revenge later on. It doesn't always work if you give in to pleas such us "Let's give him one more chance".

A talkative informant

An unpredictable employee is bad luck. An unpredictable ex-employee is a disaster, as the following story shows. In a way, it is a follow-up to the previous story because they both have a lot in common: a misunderstood fired employee with a lust for revenge and no restraint when the opportunity comes.

Place: **France**

Main characters:

Victim: Frederic, owner of a legal firm	**Former employee**: Pierre, solicitor in training

A fateful plan on a serviette

Frederic, the owner of a legal firm, couldn't believe his eyes when he arrived at work one morning. Apparently, someone had broken into their office and wrought havoc.

Papers were scattered across the tables and most of the drawers were open, their contents lying around on the floor. After a quick inspection of all the rooms in the office, it was obvious they had been burgled – they were missing a lot of things and some money.

But how come the alarm didn't go off? Did they forget to switch it on last night? Thoughts and questions were running through Frederic's head while he was waiting for the police to come. He called his employees and told them not to come to work for the time being. He was afraid they might unintentionally eliminate evidence that could lead to the capture of the burglar.

And he was quite right. The police, shortly after they started searching the crime scene, found a clue: a hand-drawn plan on a napkin from a bar. All they had to do was go there and ask the bartender who it could have belonged to. So, in just a couple of minutes they had a suspect: Pierre, a solicitor in training who had recently been fired.

When the police woke him up at his home, he couldn't remember much from the previous night. He only had a vague notion of what he had done, so they refreshed his memory with the napkin with the entrance codes and a simple sketch of the office that highlighted the places where his former colleagues kept valuable things. A red cross indicated the owner's office. And even the long numbers that were needed for opening the safe were there.

Memories of vengeance

Under the weight of evidence, Pierre recalled that the previous night in the bar he had met with a couple of small-time thieves who burgled flats and houses that he had known from before. When Pierre saw them, he got the idea of how he could take the revenge that he longed for so badly. And as he'd had a drop too much, he presented them with his plan without thinking twice. He felt like a hero in an action movie.

Pierre had felt miserable since he was dismissed. He didn't admit for a second that it could have been his fault. He thought that he did his job very well and didn't believe that they could ever find a suitable replacement for him. He was certain that his employer would soon regret firing him for no reason.

The only thing that Frederic regretted was that he'd trusted him and told him the code to the safe. And he was angry at himself for not changing all the codes, including the entrance security code, after Pierre left.

What is the lesson to be learnt?

- A bitter ex-employee will often cause you more harm than a terrible current employee. If you get rid of a troublemaker, don't assume that it's all over. Such partings often have an aftermath. This story clearly shows what **the former employee's motivation** was.

- At the same time, it is obvious what mistakes his employer made. This is a hackneyed recommendation **not to underestimate protection**. It didn't matter how expensive a security system the employer had when it was obviously so easy to misuse.

- It is the same as if you had your keys under the doormat. Remember that when an **employee with access to sensitive information** leaves your company, and take the necessary measures so that you don't one day find yourself in the position that Pierre's former employer did.

Remember:

- Make sure you protect your assets consistently: change the locks whenever anyone could have made a copy of the keys as well as all the passwords the person knows for accessing the security system.
- Don't give all employees the same PIN code - give each of them their own unique code. It is much easier to deny access to a single combination than it is to announce a change for everyone.
- Invest in monitoring: for instance, in a camera surveillance system that makes recordings. Not only will you be able to identify the offender, but any ex-employees with a chip on their shoulder will be put off "visiting" your company knowing that all your premises are monitored.

Death's messenger

How could something so dramatic have happened in a sanatorium that was opened with the purest intentions, as the only aim of its founders was to help people? Sometimes all it takes for a drama to occur is a former employee longing for revenge.

Unlike the previous stories, she decided not to harm her ex-employer, but the sanatorium clients. She blamed them and their families for her unexpected unemployment.

Place: **Spain**

Main characters:

Victims no. 1 and 2: Claudia and Fabio, the owners of a private nursing home

Victims no. 3+: clients

×

Former employee: Blanca, carer

A nursing home built with love

Claudia and Fabio had been running this particular care home for fifteen years. Their clients were retired people, some of whom were rather sprightly, enjoyed life and appreciated the agreeable surroundings of the house with its big garden, benches and lake as much as the cosy interior that looked rather like a holiday home. Besides these clients, there were also disabled people who were confined to bed. Some of them, as it seemed, had lost their sense of reality.

Hateful Blanca

The staff treated everyone with respect, as was required by their contracts. Except for Blanca. She wasn't what you'd call a good carer for people in need. She was rude and impatient; she neglected and ignored her clients. Most of them were in such a condition that they were unable to complain about her. Fortunately for them, the nurse's unusual behaviour repeatedly caught the attention of several family members who came to see their relatives and they reported her to the management.

Claudia and Fabio, who were concerned about everyone feeling comfortable, safe and respected with them, looked into the circumstances closely. After it was proved that Blanca was a character that they didn't need or want, they dismissed her without hesitation.

Growing hatred and a spiteful mission

They had no idea what trouble they would soon face because of that decision. Blanca had always hated the invalids and now she hated them even more – she had lost a job and the source of her livelihood because of them. I know, it sounds like a plot from a soap opera. Blanca, armed with knives and sharp objects, **crept into the nursing home** at around 2am when everybody was sleeping and **hurt several of them with the intention of killing them**. It was a scene like something from a horror film.

Nobody expected any intruders at that time. The doors were locked, there was a night guard at the reception and nurses in staff rooms working their night shifts. Still, Blanca managed to sneak into the building without anyone noticing her.

As a former employee, she knew the nursing home very well, including an escape route through a back door with a safety code. And since **nobody thought they should change the code after one employee was dismissed**, Blanca had an open door. Once she got in, she moved around the premises with confidence.

Fortunately, her ex-colleagues stopped her before she could actually kill anyone, but she still managed to hurt several patients, as I've mentioned. The police report later revealed that Blanca had no regrets for what she did, nor for getting arrested. The only thing she felt bad about was that she hadn't accomplished her deadly mission as she'd planned.

Becoming a patient herself

The incident revealed that **she was suffering from a serious mental health disorder** and, ironically, Blanca became a patient at the very same institution she had attacked. It may seem unjust that the staff there handled her in a very civilized way, with due respect and professionalism, although they all knew what she'd done. After all, she kept it no secret.

She was disdainful and negative towards the people who were once her colleagues, just as she had treated her patients before. She didn't display any signs of reasonableness, regret or gratitude. Of course, that was all down to her mental health issues, which nobody had known about before. **Too bad her employers didn't put her through psychological screening before they hired her**. A lot of people could have been spared a dreadful experience.

What is the lesson to be learnt?

- In fields that include working with people (not necessarily only in health care), it should be **a matter of course that new employees undergo thorough psychological testing**. As I have described in previous stories, experts in psychology can do a tremendous job and notice things that could escape the attention of a layperson's eye.

- Sophisticated examinations can reveal not only the onset of a mental health disorder, but they can also **predict or warn**, with quite a high rate of accuracy, how each employee will respond to stress in critical situations, whether they will be good team players or rather solo players, whether they are suited to working with people and what job they have the best predispositions for and so on.

- There are lot of things you can find out that may be **useful for you**, the employer, to know. With a little bit of exaggeration, it may save lives one day. And as you saw in this story, sometimes even literally.

Remember:

- Vet every applicant before holding an initial interview. At the interview, ask about every tiny detail that catches your attention or doesn't match the information in the CV.

- With applicants for more responsible positions, do psychoanalyses or tests that will tell you more about who you're actually dealing with.

- Meet with your employees regularly and ask about their health and family as well as their wishes and needs. That way, you may discover a problem early enough to help your employee as well as protect your company from future trouble.

- Don't forget about the physical surveillance of your company premises using either security staff or electronic devices. However, remember to change the entry codes.

IN CONCLUSION

I guess it will be no surprise to you when I repeat that you need to choose your employees carefully, preferably administering mental tests, but you should also take any safety measures necessary when they leave your company. Naturally, the best option is to terminate their employment amicably if you can.

Nevertheless, you can never know what may happen in the head of a jilted person who believes their dismissal was ungrounded. If such a person has any effective tools for revenge to hand, that should warn you that your security systems are insufficient.

Remember that those who take revenge ignore rules – they are driven by a certain sense of injustice, which only complicates the situation. It may pay off to offer such an employee the professional services of a psychologist who can offer a helping hand and guidance through the situation so that the employee doesn't feel wronged. There are companies that specialize in terminating employment and you can make use of their services.

Chapter XIII:

Avoiding work like the plague – a championship in procrastination

This final chapter may sound almost ironic when compared with the previous one. We still need to discuss a group of people who want everything but without doing any work. Actually, they're interested in having a cushy job that will earn them money, but they avoid the work they should be doing like the plague.

The term procrastination comes from the Latin word procrastinare. It means that a person postpones tasks and duties that need to be accomplished and does something else instead; simply said, such a person does anything except what should be done.

In the past it had a simple name: laziness. But nowadays it is considered to be almost a lifestyle disease, and the fact is that getting procrastinating employees to change their habits and start working effectively is far from easy.

Work comes last

I'm going to show you an example of procrastination in an industry where it is typical. There are lots of jokes and stories, sometimes maybe even prejudices, about the work ethics of people in the construction business. But the following story certainly has nothing to do with prejudices.

Place: **Slovakia**

Main characters:

Victim: Alexander, an employer, the boss of a construction company	×	**Employee no. 1:** Tibor, construction worker
		Employee no. 2: Blahoslav, construction worker
		Employee no. 3: Gašpar, construction worker

A group of jolly fellows

Alexander, Tibor, Gašpar and Blahoslav had worked together years ago, shortly after they left school. It was during the former communist regime, as it is nowadays referred to – real socialism. Those were the good old days for them and they always looked back in nostalgia.

Firstly, because they were young guys then, full of verve, energy and plans, and, secondly, because they weren't exactly overworked, since **it didn't matter how hard they worked, their wages were always the same**. Moreover, they brought home **a lot of "bonuses"** from building sites.

In this way, Tibor and Blahoslav got hold of various construction materials that they used at their own summer cottages. Gašpar made use of some materials when moonlighting and

Alexander renovated his flat, as well as making the flats of many of his relatives much fancier.

Those were the times of certainty for the guys. **When certitude was replaced with democracy**, they had to start working much harder. The socialist state-owned companies shattered into pieces and small entrepreneurs started popping up everywhere. Everyone suddenly wanted to have their own business. Why not, it seemed incredibly easy. Alexander established his own construction company, just as Blahoslav did. The other two friends set off into the big wide world.

Blahoslav soon came to understand that doing business didn't suit him. **Some people are born employees** – they feel much more comfortable when they're not responsible for anything or anyone and they are instead given tasks to do and don't have to worry about anything else. That's why he followed Tibor and Gašpar and found himself a job, too. Alexander was the only one who persisted, and he succeeded in building up his own company.

Meeting up after many years

I don't know exactly how, but the four of them happened to meet at Alexander's company by mere coincidence. All of them were in their fifties, and at that age it was hard to get a job.

Alexander, who had a flourishing company, **didn't want to leave his old friends high and dry**, so Tibor, Gašpar and Blahoslav teamed up again after many years.

Alexander's construction company had a good name with customers by then. Its employees were real professionals and clients knew that, so there was always enough work. That's why Alexander thought that three experienced builders would certainly come in handy.

Going back in time

What he didn't foresee was what would happen when the three friends reunited. It was as if they had gone back in time, to socialism. There's a reason for the old saying: "You can't teach an old dog new tricks". They always tried to pick a job where they'd be paid by the hour, not by the task. They knew very well that **the longer it took them, the more they would earn**.

And it usually took them quite a long time to complete anything. No wonder! They were in no particular hurry. They met up in the morning, had a coffee, chatted for a while, and then it was almost time to have lunch and two or three beers. Then they showed up where they were supposed to be, so that nobody could complain, and their working day was over. Of course, there were days when they actually worked, but even on such days they set aside a few moments to run some personal errands. There were many more days **when they just idled around**.

Sometimes the customer or manager looked for them, but they always had an explanation. Sometimes they said they'd been to fetch materials; other times they said they must have missed each other by a second or they'd had to do something urgent such as buying, changing, whatever. In fact, they were more likely to have been relaxing in the sunshine, leaning against a bag of cement.

Friend turned boss

Since Alexander's company was big, he couldn't keep an eye on every single employee. He was happy with the fact that everything went as it was supposed to and none of the customers complained.

When there was a snag or some complication every now and then, he always sorted it out in no time. But those were usually trifles, such as finding a substitute for an ill employee, adjusting deadlines or speeding up the delivery of goods. He wasn't involved in everyday operations much, as he had to direct a company and he had managers to deal with everyday issues. He was the big boss, just as he'd always wanted.

But his friends from the old days didn't see the big boss in him. For them, he was still the old Alexander who they had smoked with behind the boiler house. That may have been the reason **why they didn't pay him due respect** and they thought that nothing could happen to them. Their old friend would never sack them, would he!?

They didn't realize that the times when Alexander played cards with them instead of insulating ceilings were long gone and Alexander was in a different place now. And they didn't realize that their old friend wasn't used to receiving calls from dissatisfied customers with complaints and reminders. When Alexander found out that all the calls from angry customers were because of the trio of old friends, he didn't pull any punches. He completely floored them by presenting them with two options. Tibor, Gašpar and Blahoslav finally realized that they could either **stay and work, or pack their stuff and go**.

What is the lesson to be learnt?

- In modern times, procrastination is sometimes viewed as a diagnosis, but we're going to put this fact aside. Firstly, it hasn't been scientifically proven yet; secondly, in the context of this book we really see it as postponing actions, tasks and other things for later so that we can do something else that we find more interesting and entertaining.

- People who procrastinate often purposefully search for other things to do only to avoid doing their duties. In fact, this term reflects the times we're living in. Psychologists are now carrying out various types of research on this topic.

- Another perspective is that, these days, we call every other person who lazes around a procrastinator. It sounds better, almost academic. When I look at the previous story through this lens, I come to a clear conclusion. The employees could procrastinate because they had the opportunity. Firstly, because **nobody was supervising them**. Secondly, because **they had no deadlines to meet**. Thirdly, because **they were not motivated to perform any better**. So, they could loiter about – pardon me – procrastinate as much as they liked.

Remember:

- Whenever possible, remunerate your employees based on their achievements. Give them a low base pay and condition the rest on completing the tasks they're assigned.
- Check your employees to make sure that they are doing what they're supposed to. Do random and unannounced checks.
- Introduce the position of a controller, team leader or shift supervisor who will be responsible for the work of his or her subordinates. Trust me, if their salary is conditioned by the performance of the employees they supervise, they will certainly keep an eye on them.
- And I appeal to you yet again: dedicate enough time to selecting new employees, regardless of any past experiences you may have in common. Believe me, it pays off much more than training somebody and then parting ways with such a newcomer and looking for another one.

A professional patient

One of the most popular ways to avoid work is to simply feign illness. Unfortunately, even an employee who **is officially unfit to work over the long term** is still an employee, whether we, employers, like it or not. Even though such people don't do their jobs, we cannot simply cross out their names and act as if they don't exist, even though that would often be the best solution.

Place: **Czech Republic**

Main characters:

Victim no. 1:
owner of a company that operates on shifts

Victim no. 2:
an unjustly accused employee

×

Employee:
Jana,
an inventive employee

People are different

There may be some people who spring swiftly out of bed every morning before their alarm clock goes off and cannot wait to get back to work again. However, there are only a small number of people who enjoy their jobs, feel self-actualized and don't question their work's importance for a second, let alone have thoughts of staying in their warm beds and not going anywhere. We should admit that most of us ordinary mortals happen to think every now and then about how sweet it would be if we didn't have to go anywhere and how happy we would be if we could spend half a day lying in bed after coming up with an acceptable excuse.

And then there are employees who wish this much more often than others but, what is worse, they are able to bring their ideas to fruition. This has been epitomized in simple **malingering**. When you come across such a professional patient, it always means trouble. They're very inventive.

An intriguer

That was exactly the case with Jana who felt bored to death at work. Moreover, she had to work shifts and she didn't like that at all. She would have quit the job, but she couldn't afford to be unemployed. So what was the way out?

She was ill suspiciously often, so her employer **called her doctor to find out what her diagnosis was**. Logically, the doctor didn't want to cover for her fake illnesses. She could break an arm or leg, she thought, but she rejected the idea immediately as she liked herself too much to harm herself.

Jana didn't admit she was doing anything wrong, she blamed the bothersome job. But to be honest, **Jana found every job troublesome after doing it for a couple of days**. It was probably due to a bad choice of work, unlucky coincidence or ironic twist of fate, she thought. She considered herself flawless. She just desperately didn't want to go to work. She hated getting up early in the morning, she was unhappy with how long her working hours were, she didn't like afternoon shifts and she couldn't stand night shifts. She thought that the heavens must be against her.

Be careful what you wish for

She wished, for so long, that she wouldn't have to go to work – that is, until it happened. Jana told her bosses that a colleague she worked with on night shift had raped her at work. Consequently, she was given several weeks off work for recovery and nobody questioned that.

She claimed that she was feeling ashamed and stressed because of the terrible experience, so hadn't reported it immediately, when evidence could have been gathered, but two days later, after she failed to show up for her shift.

Everyone understood that Jana couldn't go to work in such an emotional state and that taking sick leave was absolutely appropriate.

An unexpected conclusion

The employer and the police couldn't make light of her accusation. Especially when she was in such terrible mental condition that she couldn't even go to work.

The police looked into the case very thoroughly. They checked all the details, interrogated Jana, the suspect, witnesses and other colleagues, and the company owner willingly disclosed **recordings from the security cameras installed on the premises**.

That was something Jana didn't consider. Unfortunately for her, **the investigation clearly revealed that she'd made up everything**. She didn't know the colleague very well, she had accused him randomly, she had no qualms about her behaviour and **didn't care what would happen to him in the slightest**.

She naively thought that no one would do anything about it – that others would only feel sorry for her and that she could stay home for some time. This was the only wish that actually came true: she didn't have to go back to work again, nobody was interested in seeing her there. She was immediately given the sack and was investigated by the police for false accusation.

What is the lesson to be learnt?

- **Scams involving sick leave** are a common vice on the part of employees. Sick leave is misused particularly by workers who use the time when they are officially ill to moonlight and gain extra income.

- It happens rather frequently that somebody **starts a new job planning that** after the probation period ends **they will hand in a sick note** and receive long-term benefits.

Remember:

▶ If an employee is ill too often, it should warn you that something is probably wrong.

▶ Being an employer, you are entitled to check up on your employees when they are ill. If you find out that they are not at the address where they stated they would be, you're entitled to have the matter investigated by the relevant authorities that may revoke their sick leave.

▶ As I've mentioned, salaries should be based on the actual work your employees do: that way, it won't be advantageous for them to stay at home. Although, I must admit that it is not always possible.

Full-time union members

Some employees can read between the lines very well and find extra benefits there. Sometimes a benefit that you find hard to believe. The following story is about two men who perfected reading between the lines.

You are likely to doubt that it actually happened. Even I was taken aback by the absurdity. But I can tell you, it is a true story and I didn't make up a single word of it.

Place: **Italy**

Main characters:

Victim:
Manuel,
owner
of a hotel chain

Employee no. 1:
Marco,
gardener
and self-sacrificing
union member

Employee no. 2:
Alberto,
maintenance man
and self-sacrificing
union member

A successful entrepreneur

Manuel's network of hotels was expanding. He was proud that his business was doing so well. When he started with a small family bed and breakfast fifteen years before, he didn't even dream that he would expand beyond the boundaries of his small maritime village. But now his company had hotels on the peninsula as well as on small islands near the coast. Naturally, he had a rather large number of employees.

Union members everywhere

Marco and Alberto were old friends. Manuel had hired Marco ten years ago as a gardener for one of his hotels and, after some time, Alberto got a job there as a maintenance man. They had both joined the union shortly after getting their jobs. There was nothing strange about it, not even the fact that they **read the statutes and agreements** signed by them and their boss.

The strange thing was how they misinterpreted them and how inventive they were when taking advantage of that. The statutes specified that every employee was entitled to spend several hours each month **working for the trade union**. And what's more, if one employee didn't use up their time, **another employee was entitled to do the work instead**.

One thing led to another and the gardener–maintenance man duo **became full-time union members**. Surprisingly, they got away with that trick for several years and all the actual work had to be done by their colleagues from another shift. They did some useful work from time to time so as not to evoke suspicion.

When all of that came to light, by coincidence, they were not able to specify exactly what activity they actually did instead of the work they were being paid for. Only one thing was for sure: **they had used the hours left unused by their colleagues who hadn't come up with the same idea as them**.

A surprising end

It is paradoxical how this story ended. Marco and Alberto hired a seasoned attorney who came to the conclusion that they had acted within the union agreement signed by their employer of his own free will.

According to the lawyer, who also excelled at reading between the lines, **the employer should pay both employees**, even if they carried on with their full-time work for the trade union, simply because they would be doing nothing illegal. Manuel didn't expect such a conclusion and he definitely wasn't going to accept it.

Nevertheless, getting rid of the two most active trade union workers wasn't as easy as he had imagined and it required a lot of effort before he succeeded in dismissing them. You see, trade unions are very, very serious organizations. After all, their mission is to fight for employees' interests as hard as they can.

What is the lesson to be learnt?

- Have all **agreements, their amendments and other documents** that you conclude with your employees **written up by experts** who will make sure that they are bulletproof against inventive employees who could strip you of your money without delivering much work. **The relationship between the employer and the employee has to be legally well defined**. Remember that clear provisions in employment contracts may help you avoid many undesirable surprises.

- At the same time, the good old advice – **check**, check, check – is also appropriate here. You too may have companies or branches dispersed in many places, and you think it is impossible to supervise every single employee, especially if they work in another corner of the country. But as I've written many times, don't underestimate the power and reach of control mechanisms.

- I've also suggested and described quite a few alternatives as to how you can **keep track of what your employees are doing**. You can certainly pick the one that suits you best. **You definitely shouldn't rely on the automatic loyalty of your employees without supervision**.

Remember:

- ▶ A good lawyer is priceless, not only when it comes to dealing with disputes, but also when writing your company's rules, regulations and employment contracts.
- ▶ Here too, you should follow the previously-mentioned simple advice: pay your employees for the work that they actually do, meaning per task. Then it doesn't pay off to procrastinate, whatever their way of avoiding their work duties is.

Experimental workplace

Surprisingly, employees in some fields may be more efficient when they are given more flexibility and can work from home. The positive effects of working from home have been confirmed by multiple studies carried out on this topic in the USA and Europe. It might be an inspiration for you, too.

It was a similar study that inspired the owner of a travel agency who, together with a certain unnamed university that carried out the research, let several of his employees from the call centre work from home for some time. You can read about how that ended in the following story.

Place: **United Kingdom**

Main characters:

Victim: Jim, the owner of a travel agency	×	**Employee no. 1:** Sheldon, call centre manager **Employees no. 2+:** Sheldon's subordinates in the call centre

Jim's modest beginnings

Jim thought of himself as a modern person who keeps up with the times and he was open to innovations. It was probably thanks to his good intuition, or a lucky coincidence, that all the changes he had ever made eventually paid off.

The travel agency that he had established a few years before had high ambitions and was flourishing as planned. It was very competitive and in quite a short time it grew from a "garage" firm with a handful of employees into a big company with a good reputation and several hundred employees, which was quite something.

I must say that Jim was a good employer. He was able to motivate his employees and they were very loyal to him. What they valued most was the fact that although he was the big boss of a large company, he was willing to listen to anyone who came to him with a problem or proposal for improvement. As Jim insisted on an open labour policy, he sometimes came to hear that some of his employees weren't working as they should be.

Lazy guys with headsets

When Jim found out how many of his call centre employees spent half of their working hours sitting at their desks with a coffee and snacks exchanging funny stories, he had to think about what to do. He was a down-to-earth person who never got carried away by emotions and always thoroughly analysed every situation. Only after thinking through the possible options and their consequences did he act.

He decided not to make any rash decisions and not to dismiss the underperforming employees. He was taking his time to think it through, when he was contacted by a prestigious university that invited him to take part in an experiment that was currently underway. The experiment was aimed at assessing how much work productivity and employee morale rose or fell when employees were allowed to work from home. As always, Jim thought the offer through, and he eventually agreed to it. He selected the call centre employees for the project, who, according to his information, didn't work 100 per cent of their working hours.

Uneasiness about the experiment

Sheldon, the call centre manager, left the meeting with his boss with a head full of questions. He wasn't sure whether the employees he felt responsible for would do even at least the same amount of work as before without his supervision.

What if they did whatever they liked instead of work? What if it got him into trouble as the person in charge of the call centre? What if they didn't try hard or at all, since they were already able to chat for half the day despite being in full sight?

Sheldon felt uneasy about it. Frankly, he didn't share his superior's excessive optimism regarding their work ethics or morale. Moreover, his boss strictly forbade him to tell them that if they failed to achieve at least the same results as they had up until then – when they were procrastinating merrily – they would have to search for work elsewhere. How the heck was he to motivate them?

The world of homeworking

The selected telephonists had mixed feelings when they heard the news. Some of them were enthused. There were even some who said that they'd longed for something like that. Others were nonplussed: they didn't have much faith in themselves. They doubted that they would actually do any work at all if they didn't have to.

Consequently, it wasn't that simple. They all had to work. Sheldon handed them Jim's weekly plan in which he defined what results he expected them to deliver by the end of the week. That was all. No detailed breakdown, no supervision or random check. All of them were masters of their own time and it was totally up to them when and how they performed the scheduled tasks. They would have a chance to show what they were really worth.

A study with a happy ending

This was repeated week in week out. To everyone's surprise, the productivity of the employees working from home improved in the first month by 13 per cent. Moreover, they were less frequently ill (or they didn't pretend to be ill when they could plan their day as they needed) and Jim's procrastination problem disappeared.

When the experiment was over after a couple of months, the conclusions to be drawn were obvious. The team of employees working from home had better results than those who went to work and had regular working hours. Then an incredible thing happened. You don't have to believe it, but I swear to God it really was so. Jim allowed all his employees to work from home whenever they wanted. And he added that everyone would be paid according to the results achieved, not according to where they did the work.

Some of the employees were happy to make use of the offer, others preferred to work from the company's office. Jim supported all their decisions, although he made sure that everyone knew that they would lose their privileges and a benevolent employer if they didn't perform their tasks by the prescribed deadlines.

What is the lesson to be learnt?

- As I mentioned at the beginning of this story, there have been several studies conducted in the USA and Europe on the topic of increased work productivity when working from home. The results show that almost half of employees think that **they are more successful and creative if they can choose where they work from**. More than a third of the population said that they longed for this option.

- Generally, studies have shown that in fields where this type of working arrangement is possible and can be applied in practice, it brings better results. It decreases the risk of employee procrastination.

- What plays a key role here is the **advanced technology** that makes working from home possible. It's also come out that members of the young generation that have just entered the labour market in particular have a different notion of employment and their place of work than previous generations. Therefore, we can expect the new generation to pioneer this new dimension of employment.

Remember:

- Selecting the method of delivering work is always subject to agreement between the employer and employees, however, it is restricted by the nature of the work itself. If you opt for having employees working from home, it brings with it certain advantages (savings on employee-related costs, an interesting benefit in many employers' eyes) as well as specific duties for both parties involved.
- With this model of work, both parties understand that performance comes before hours worked. That means that the employees are more motivated to complete their tasks.
- Employees save time by not commuting to work, and often they actually work longer than they would in the office. Nevertheless, thorough control is appropriate in the form of conference calls and checking the work actually done.

IN CONCLUSION

If employees don't want to work, their inventiveness in how to avoid work knows no boundaries. It is again a question of your control as to whether and for how long they can get away with such an attitude. You can try to motivate them more, or look for somebody else who's more interested in doing the work for you.

It also depends on what the current unemployment rate is in your country as well as on the characteristics of each employee. Sometimes an exemplary dismissal of the least efficient employee may increase the efficiency of the team. However, you should always proceed with the utmost caution and assess each individual case in a wider context so that you don't dismiss an important link without which the entire chain will collapse.

CONCLUSION

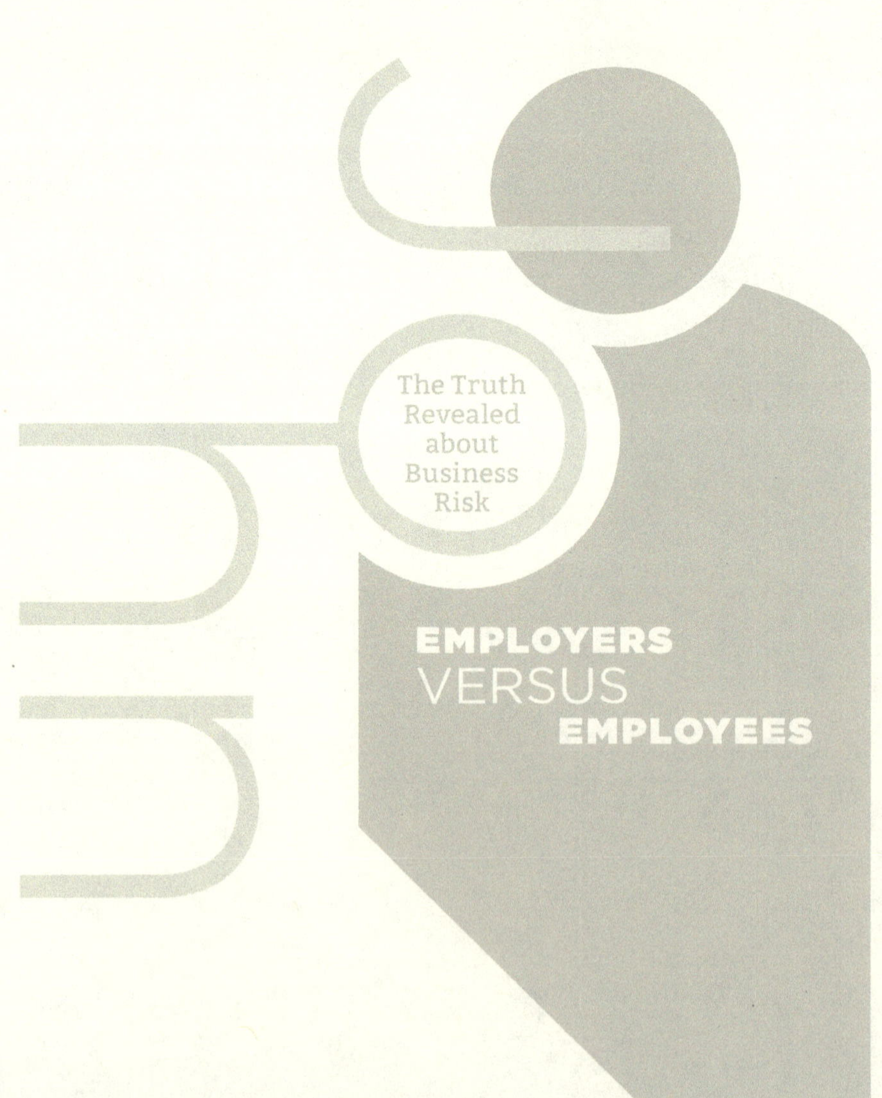

The Truth
Revealed
about
Business
Risk
EMPLOYERS
VERSUS
EMPLOYEES

The stories in this book actually happened. Many similar stories are currently happening and they always will. In conclusion, I would like to sum up the facts and give you some tips and advice in order to decrease the likelihood that you will become a deceived employer one day.

Appendix I: Association of Certified Fraud Examiners (ACFE)

The **ACFE** is an international association that investigates, among other things, fraud committed by employees. Annual surveys conducted by this association evidence that it is a problem on a worldwide scale. The ACFE **defines fraud** as "the use of one's occupation for personal gain through the deliberate misuse or misapplication of the organization's resources or assets." The ACFE has also revealed that, paradoxically, theft and fraud occur much more frequently in small companies that don't pay as much attention to supervision as large companies do, which makes them more vulnerable.

The ACFE distinguishes **three main types of occupational fraud**:

1. **Asset misappropriation** – this includes tangible and intangible assets. Asset misappropriation concerns theft of any kind, loans or phony payments. Intangible assets include primarily intellectual property. In this case, misappropriation

is everything from abuse or theft of documentation to computer criminality and industrial espionage.

2. **Corruption** – I suppose I don't have to explain what this encompasses. We all know that it concerns bribery, or accepting bribes, inducing or participating in fraud and – last but not least – money laundering.

3. **Financial statement fraud** – there is a wide range of possible ways in which fraud can be committed: from deliberately false statements about revenues and expenses to incorrectly reported asset values to disguising various financial machinations. Financial and accounting scams still rank at the top in statistics.

According to the latest research, the ACFE has compiled the following simplified guidelines on **how to avoid risks** or at least manage them.

1. **Anti-corruption hotline** – the ACFE bases its recommendations on findings according to which up to 40 per cent of fraud was revealed thanks to an anonymous source or report. In most cases it came out that the notifier was another employee. In this case **anonymity** is justified and beneficial, as many people still think that if they report others' mistakes or offences, they will become snitches, squealers or rats (pick any word you like). They fear that their allegations will only cause them trouble, cause them to lose the trust of their colleagues and lead to retribution. Naturally, there's the other side of anonymity. Experience has shown that when people are encouraged to report problems **anonymously** and **with a promise of remuneration**, many **false accusations** are made only with a view to easy money.

2. **Warning signs** – according to research, up to 90 per cent of offenders showed common characteristics. Some warning signs are when employees **live beyond their means**, have **financial problems**, have close **relationships with customers** or are **unwilling to share their duties** with others and even **refuse inspections** and **days off**.

3. **Audits** – experience has shown that **internal audits** are much more effective than external audits, which – according to statistics – reveal only 3 per cent of all fraud. This suggests that your focus should be on establishing **control mechanisms inside your company**.

4. **Prevention** – although it may seem like a useless investment, you shouldn't **underestimate prevention**. Losses usually exceed prevention costs many times over. **Verify the information presented** by job applicants, require them to submit **a copy of their criminal record** and define **clear rules** for all departments.

5. **Supervision** – even if you define the above-mentioned preventive measures at the very start, you certainly shouldn't underestimate control mechanisms as you go. **Monitoring vehicles, phone calls and what your employees do on computers at work** is part of a reasonable entrepreneur's routine. You should install **surveillance cameras** everywhere where employees can steal your goods or cause other serious damage.

6. **Emergency plan** – if you happen to reveal a fraudulent employee, you should proceed according to an emergency plan that **has been approved beforehand** by the company's competent authorities and that defines who is to

conduct **the investigation**, what **qualifications** this person or team is to have, what **the objective of the investigation** is to be and what the **consequences** will be for the person under investigation. In case of serious offences, **co-operation with the police** should also be defined and – if the situation requires – **informing the public** of the results of the investigation. Naturally, the last part isn't meant for minor offences, such as when you catch an employee making a private call.

7. **Anticipation** – have each employee sign a bulletproof contractual agreement for all possible cases: **material liability, a confidentiality agreement, a non-competitive clause**. Anticipate what may happen if you part ways not exactly on good terms.

8. **Ethical code** – even though I am mentioning this term last, it should be the **alpha and omega** of your business. **Rules clearly defining** how everyone in the company should behave and what sanctions they will face in case of a breach and what the employer isn't willing to tolerate or accept should never be missing from any company. Such a simple thing can save you a lot of unexpected trouble.

Forensic and investigation services

Leaving the minor offences of employees working for small companies aside, as I'm sure you, employers, can cope with them, I'd like to dedicate a little space to those who have larger companies or bigger problems with employees. In many cases, it is not within such companies' powers to investigate "mere" allegations and gather a **sufficient amount** of conclusive **evidence**. Fraudulent employees, scared by the vision of a trial, end up just quitting their jobs. I must warn you: you shouldn't settle with that! Otherwise you're indirectly signalling to other employees that although some John Doe embezzled a rather large sum, not much happened to him anyway.

I presume that most of you don't employ a team of experienced and trained investigators. There's no need to. You can hire **external specialists** who will render their professional services whenever needed. The essentials of forensic and investigation services are **speed, experience and collaboration** with the client conditioned by **the auditor's confidentiality**. After a thorough analysis, including interviews with all persons concerned, you are given **a report** that will contain not only **evidence** (or **suspicion**) of the illegal activity of any of your employees (*what happened, who did it and what circumstances led to it*), but also **proposed measures** that you should take in order to prevent such a situation from happening again in the future.

You can assess the degree of risk linked with each employee using psychological forensic auditing (PFA). PFA focuses primarily on the following spheres: what job the employee is currently doing, how high up in the hierarchy the employee is, what means the employee has at hand, what company interests the employee may jeopardize, what material and financial conditions the employee has and what control mechanisms are being applied in relation to the employee. The information is complemented with some personal aspects of the employees' life that could influence potentially risky conduct.

Prevention

FPA is suitable for preventive **risk assessment**. When it comes to prevention, the research is divided into two categories: structural and dynamic.

The structural analysis focuses, among other things, on what the **company interests** and **priorities** are and in what sphere there's a **real risk** of financial, material or information damage. The analysis also deals with the **system of protection** of these company interests, **defines** what is considered to be **in breach** and what **consequences or punishment** shall ensue.

The dynamic analysis examines employees' **predispositions** to **risky and dishonest behaviour**. It focuses closely on **individuals**, their **motivations**, **professional targets**, the use of their **abilities**, how they **behave** in critical or mentally difficult situations and many other aspects. Thanks to this you can get a picture of what your employees are like and how they could behave should they get in an unusual situation. Below I describe what else you can learn.

Basic types of employees

Generally speaking, we can distinguish between four types of employees. Let's start with the ideal one.

1. **An honest employee** – a person who is **honest and loyal** under any circumstances and dishonest conduct is out of the question.

2. **An employee that fails in a crisis** – a person who **doesn't resist temptation or opportunity** when in a critical or extreme life situation but hopes, or expects, to make things right after everything gets back on the right track.

3. **A rational dishonest employee** – a person who immediately and without hesitation uses an opportunity to **deliberately embezzle assets** after rationally assessing the risk of getting caught.

4. **A pathological dishonest employee** – a person who (usually repeatedly) behaves **dishonestly regardless of the risk** of getting caught.

Selecting employees

It's beyond any doubt that all of you desire to have only employees of the first type. But how can you tell if you're dealing with such an honest employee? If we could rely on our own intuitions and they never betrayed us, we would be safe. Then there would be no reason for me to write this book, as there simply wouldn't be anything to write about. In reality, there are more employees who are far from being perfect than one would expect.

Therefore, I have a suggestion for you, and it is entirely up to you what you do with it. When selecting new employees, you can be greatly helped by psychology. Yes, **a psychological profile** can reveal a lot, and it is no secret that today it is a normal part of the recruitment process in many companies. **Good psychological tests** that focus on more than just **personality questionnaires** and the **intelligence** of the applicants should reveal much more. They can provide you with a **risk assessment** for each applicant, estimate what their **work performance** will be like, whether they are prone to **(dis) loyalty, aggression** or **bullying**, what attitude they will have in **critical situations**, if they are able to **cooperate, manage people** and what their **attitude towards authority** is.

Online tests

You can even try to give your future as well as current employees special tests, some of which can be taken online. **Such questionnaires** are usually created by a team of psychologists.

However, they're taken without human interaction and assessed mechanically. Therefore, these tests should assess – on the basis of psychological profiling – the **likelihood** that an employee will behave in a way harmful to the employer. Nevertheless, even their authors admit that **the result** that you will get is only **approximate** and the questionnaires aren't a substitute for the work of an experienced psychologist or an excellent HR manager. Psychological experts recommend **combining** these tests **with other methods**.

Appendix II: Data protection

A specific problem that could harm your business interests is the **theft or misuse of company data**. That's why I've decided to include an appendix on this topic.

It's no secret that knowhow is stored in company data and information systems. Statistics show that you don't have to fear attacks from the outside as much as attacks from disloyal employees. The numbers are quite clear. Hacker attacks from the outside account for no more than 14 per cent of all attacks, the rest are made by employees. Their data theft and abuse accounts for 12 per cent of all attacks. True, it is less than the 14 per cent of attacks made by hackers; however, employees are responsible for the loss of data carriers, while 50 per cent cause damage to their employers through negligence.

A high-risk group of employees are those who are leaving your company. Many of them tend to take internal data and information along. In most cases, they are aware of it and they intend to sell the information or use it to the benefit of the competition. Some of them, and this is rather strange, don't even do so in bad faith. Typically, these are people who contributed to the creation of the data and they suppose wrongly that they have the right to use it, totally ignoring the logic that everything created under their employment contract is the intellectual property of the company or owners, not the employees.

How to protect your data

1. **By introducing rules** – rules concerning handling data should be part of the contract that you sign with employees. Clearly state that the rules are binding and what sanctions employees face in case of their breach.

2. **Thorough surveillance** – let's be honest. Almost nothing can work without thorough control of how the rules are adhered to. So your employees might not consider a security clause so binding unless they know someone is making sure that they act accordingly.

Naturally, by such control I don't mean shadowing employees, catching them by surprise or hiring a private eye who would spy on them outside working hours. A much smarter and efficient form of control is log assessment. If you want to keep perfect track of what your employees do with your data, you shouldn't allow them to use it on their personal devices. If you allow BYOD (bring your own device), you should make sure that your employees are familiar with the security rules to the last detail.

3. **Data security** – use the technologies available, including encryption tools, changing passwords on a regular basis and the like. Define degrees of authority and divide them

among more people, while only authorized persons should have access to sensitive information. It is always important to classify data by setting rules that define who can handle what data, under what conditions and how and where the data can be transferred.

Most frequently stolen data

According to international research, the most frequently stolen data are as follows:

1) information on companies' economic results,
2) data on bank cards,
3) information on offers presented in tenders,
4) accounting data and
5) trade secrets – offers, lists of customers.

The most common failures and inappropriate behaviour on the part of employees

Data theft is often caused by the negligence of employees who don't have anything to do with the theft itself. They "only" facilitate, albeit unwittingly, thieves' access to information. The typical failures are as follows:

1) not keeping the office secured,

2) placing agreements or sensitive data on tables or in folders (not in an archive or locked in a case),

3) leaving a computer that is not password protected unattended,

4) storing company data on private devices that are not sufficiently protected (desktop computers, laptops, mobile phones, tablets, clouds, for example) and

5) toring access passwords, codes and keys on personal devices. In extreme cases, even writing them on papers, sticky notes and the like that are in visible places near their computers, often even stuck to them.

Appendix III: Procrastination and precrastination

Procrastination

According to statistics, the average employee wastes up to **two hours a day** on the Internet. And that still sounds rather optimistic. You might want to know what that means in terms of money.

This wasted time costs the average company **about 10,000 dollars per year**. That doesn't seem very good when you multiply it by the number of your employees, does it?

However, employees don't "idle" only at the workplace. Research has shown that more and more employees deliberately make doctors' appointments during working hours, spend less time there than they report to their employers and make up various excuses and reasons for arriving late, leaving early or not showing up at all. A survey on this topic conducted with top managers from various companies showed that 84 per cent of them have experienced such employee behaviour.

All of this shirking has recently been hidden under the term *procrastination*. As I've mentioned before, it cannot be used as an excuse or explanation for employee absenteeism and I consider it unfortunate that it can be a label for a diagnosis that needs to be shown consideration.

The truth is that procrastination doesn't always have to be perceived as negative. Some people work harder when motivated by an approaching deadline. They become more efficient as the adrenaline grows, while it would take them three times as long otherwise. Naturally, this may only be applied to certain fields and under certain conditions. It usually concerns creative and freelance professions. Therefore, if employees are given flexibility and they accomplish their tasks without deadlines or any complications and there's nothing they can be criticized for, then it would be unreasonable to force them to change a working process that suits them. The result is always what matters most.

Several books have been published on the topic of procrastination. You can even attend lectures and training on how to fight it. Of course, the quality and usefulness varies and is conditioned by the organizer's experience. If you decide to make use of some of these options, choose carefully and pick respectable lecturers.

Precrastination

The term *precrastination* is not that common yet. Still, I believe I don't need to explain to you at length what it means. You probably know or can guess that it is the opposite of procrastination.

One might think that a proactive employee is a godsend for every employer. I should warn you here: not always. Too much activeness can be to the detriment of the cause. Employees (and people in general) who thrust themselves into work immediately and rashly are not ideal either. It often happens that such employees eagerly complete a job long before the deadline, but the conditions or the assignment later change and all the work they did suddenly proves worthless, which means that even the time spent on that job was not used efficiently. Probably, the only benefit is that the employee can feel the satisfaction of getting the work done on time and not having been bored. But that's about all.

But, for the most part, employees who precrastinate feel angry, desperate and that their effort is not sufficiently appreciated, without realizing that they're partly to blame. Every mediocre training session on labour efficiency teaches how important it is to define a task accurately and precisely so that employees understand it fully and to define a schedule before its implementation actually starts.

This implies that even when employees frantically get to work, it is not exactly a contribution. Psychological studies have shown that the perfect employee is somewhere half-way between the procrastinator and the precrastinator.

If you want to get a rough estimate of which way your employees lean, you can make use of tests focused on this topic. By answering a series of interlinked questions, you can come to conclusions about what your employees are inclined to do or naturally predisposed to. The questions may be something like this:

What would you do if...

... a lot of duties piled up and you weren't able to manage anymore?

... a new episode of your favourite series were aired, but you were supposed to work at that time?

... you didn't feel like getting down to a complicated task?

These are just a few examples of what you could come across on the test. Of course, they include even more personal questions – for instance: When do you buy Christmas presents? You will get clear results indicating where each employee ranks between procrastination and precrastination.

POSTFACE

It is only up to you, dear entrepreneurs and employers in one. If you don't anticipate business risk, including the occupational risks that are discussed in this book, you're likely to face smaller or bigger problems for your business, or even such that may prove fatal.

However, in such cases your bad or greedy employees won't be the only people to blame. You'll need to search for the original mistake in the person who could have prevented their misconduct but didn't do so. Yes, you will be the one who allowed or tolerated such conduct and who wasn't careful enough.

Be observant, take an interest in new trends in fighting occupational risks, talk to experts and trust me, all of these risks can be tamed. Remember, I'm on your side and I'm here to give you advice on how to cope with various risks in various fields of business, also in the future.

Stay tuned.
Yours, Vladimir John.

Note:
To protect the privacy of certain individuals and companies their namesand identifying details have been changed.

EMPLOYERS VERSUS EMPLOYEES

Vladimir John

Publisher
MERIGLOBE ADVISORY HOUSE Ltd.
Nwms Center, 31 Southampton Row
Office 3.11, 3rd Floor
London, WC1B 5HJ
United Kingdom.

Translation Vít Prošek,
proofreading Rebecca Hollinger,
copy-editing Francesca White,
Redit Publishing Services.
Graphic Layout J. Bartoš.
Printed and bound
by Finidr, Český Těšín.

ISBN 978-1-911511-52-6

www.ingramcontent.com/pod-product-compliance
Lightning Source LLC
LaVergne TN
LVHW041114080826
845145LV00007B/1813

* 9 7 8 1 9 1 1 5 1 1 5 2 6 *